Costume:
THE PERFORMING PARTNER

by **JAC LEWIS** and
MIRIAM STRIEZHEFF LEWIS

illustrated by
JAC LEWIS

foreword by
JULIE HARRIS

mp
MERIWETHER PUBLISHING LTD.
Colorado Springs, Colorado

Meriwether Publishing Ltd., Publisher
P.O. Box 7710
Colorado Springs, CO 80933

Executive Editor: Arthur L. Zapel
Book design: Tom Myers
Illustrations: Jac Lewis
Artwork for cover: Arthur L. Zapel
Typesetting: Cheryl Tuder

© Copyright MCMXC Meriwether Publishing Ltd.
Printed in the United States of America
First Edition
Library of Congress #90-53279

Library of Congress Cataloging-in-Publication Data

Lewis, Jac.
    Costume: the performing partner / by Jac Lewis and Miriam Striezheff Lewis ; foreword by Julie Harris — 1st ed.
       p.   cm.
    Includes bibliographical references and index.
    ISBN 0-916260-71-2
    1. Costume. I. Lewis, Miriam Striezheff. II. Title.
PN2067.L49   1990
792'.026--dc20   90-53279
                                                             CIP

In celebration of our parents

Mark and Fannie Lewis
Joseph and Rae Striezheff

Table of Contents

Julie Harris as Mary Todd Lincoln
in her inaugural gown in The Last of Mrs. Lincoln.

Foreword

Theatre costumes always excite me, both as an actress and as part of the audience.

As *Costume: The Performing Partner* points out, an actor receives inspiration even from an improvised costume or a small accessory. One of the first plays I was in in New York City was a comedy, *Magnolia Alley*. I was playing a little Southern sort-of-Cinderella girl who made the beds and washed the dishes. To make me "feel" right I put on over my cotton dress an apron my Grandmother Smith had made. It was faded from many washings and felt perfect.

In Bessie Breuer's *Sundown Beach* once again I played a poor Southern girl. Since it was a modern story, Elia Kazan, who was directing the play, asked us to bring things from home which we would think appropriate. I brought an old cotton skirt — I never throw away anything — but Lenka Peterson, who was also in the play, helped make my costume just right by bringing me a shirt her grandmother had made many years before.

This book covers the importance of the influence of color and fabric upon an actor's performance. My black dress, saucy black velvet hat and colored chiffon scarf made me really feel like Sally Bowles in John van Druten's *I Am a Camera*. The white dress, copied from the original one that is still hanging in Emily Dickinson's bedroom in the Homestead, Amherst, Massachusetts, helped me to recreate her character. In *A Shot in the Dark* I wanted to look like Brigitte Bardot. The simple little black dress I wore was copied from my own — very clingy, with a low neckline — and I even felt I had to wear French perfume.

I can still see the faded lavender robe Laurette Taylor wore when she served breakfast coffee to her son Tom in Tennessee Williams' *The Glass Menagerie*. The book's anecdote of Miss Taylor's last-minute decision to change the color of her robe the opening night of the play demonstrates how important the appropriate color was for both her mood and the audience's reaction to the emotion of the scene. I have the enduring impression, too, of Judith Anderson as *Medea* in Robinson Jeffers' play, her barbaric

1

robes reinforcing the strength and intensity of her performance.

The costume helps to shape the portrayal of a character. Putting on my hoopskirts in James Prideaux's play *The Last of Mrs. Lincoln*, I became President Lincoln's wife, just as I turned into the adolescent Frankie Addams in *The Member of the Wedding* the moment I put on a pair of shorts and padded around barefooted.

Why does one person dress differently from someone else? Because each person has a unique quality. That's the fun of life. We don't wear uniforms as a rule and, even if we did, our own style would make the same uniform look slightly dissimilar on each of us.

Costume: The Performing Partner stresses the value of research. I love to pore over art books, go to art museums, and read about the real people I have been asked to portray on stage and in movies. Before I appeared as Emily Dickinson in *The Belle of Amherst*, I made a pilgrimage to Amherst, Massachusetts. To prepare for my role as Charlotte Brontë I journeyed to the Brontë parsonage in Haworth, Yorkshire, England. To understand as much as possible the life of Mrs. Lincoln, I visited Mary and Abraham Lincoln's home in Springfield, Illinois. I even went to Lexington, Kentucky where Mary Lincoln once lived. Although her home is no longer there, it was lovely and inspirational to see the town.

I find Jac and Miriam Lewis' book, *Costume: The Performing Partner*, very lively and stimulating, making the actor's use of the costume an important and exciting aspect of theatre art. The book presents a new concept of the costume and, with its combination of theatre history, will serve as a wonderful guide to the beginning actor, and a stimulant to any professional actor.

Everything evokes feelings in you, and you never know what will be the exciting right thing — so you must keep searching — and this book will point the way.

Julie Harris

Preface

While Anne Baxter was appearing on Broadway in *Noël Coward in Two Keys*, I spoke to her of my intention to write a book concerning costume in relation to the actor's performance. A few days after her enthusiastic reaction, I received the following note from her:

"An actor's costume does far more than clothe the actor. It becomes the peculiar carapace, or even second skin, into which one climbs and, as one does so, feels a character quicken. How wonderful that you have recognized the extraordinary importance of costuming to the live core of an actor's performance."

My first recognition of the importance of the costume to the actor and its profound influence upon the acting of the performer occurred in 1939, while working as staff designer at Eaves Costume Company, then located on West 46th Street in New York.

During my lunch hour breaks I would try on Napoleonic coats, eighteenth-century jackets, Elizabethan capes, hats and helmets of various periods. Each costume or its accessory stirred within me an emotion that transported me back in time. I would ask myself, "If I sense a change in my own emotions, how does an actor respond when he sees himself for the first time completely costumed for his new role?"

At Eaves I watched many of the great actors and actresses of our American theatre being fitted in costumes: among them, Katharine Cornell, Clifton Webb, Tallulah Bankhead, and the eminent Otis Skinner visiting Eaves with his daughter, Cornelia Otis Skinner. Each one of these experienced actors instinctively knew the importance of every detail of the costume he was to wear.

In addition to the actors coming to Eaves were producers, directors and costume designers. The producer-director, John Murray Anderson, was working with Billy Rose on the 1939 World's Fair Aquacade, while Raoul Pene Du Bois designed the costumes. In Du Bois' costume creations, he demonstrated the impact of color upon the actor as well as upon the audience.

3

I was excited by costume designer Irene Sharaff's creativity and her use of vibrant colors in costumes for the original musical production of Balanchine's *On Your Toes* with Ray Bolger and the ballet dancer, Tamara Geva. This musical comedy preceded Agnes de Mille's ballets for *Oklahoma!* and was the first to have ballet as an integral part of the plot. Balanchine and de Mille understood the value of the response of the dancer as well as the actor to the costume.

Observing the fine actors and designers who entered Eaves' doors and set the standard for those who followed them, my belief was strengthened in the relationship between the actor and the costume, and the important influence the costume has upon an actor's performance.

Through my years of designing for all the performing arts, the multiple uses of the costume led me to the conclusion that the costume is as important an aid to the actor as all the other tools necessary to his complete development. The costume not only delineates a character, it influences the actor's posture, movement, mood and understanding of the role. The actor must learn to use the costume as a reflection of the character's personality and situation, recognizing and utilizing the reaction it evokes within the performer.

August Strindberg, in the foreword to his play, *Miss Julie*, wrote: "Like almost all other art, that of the stage has long seemed to me a sort of *Biblia Pauperum*, or a Bible in pictures for those who cannot read what is written or printed." The visual experience is the medium of today. Its power and value is timeless and limitless, and influences the actor as well as the audience.

The theatre is a major element of our heritage, and within it the costume holds title to a definitive and necessary role. Its influence upon the actor is manifold, and the various facets of costume must be fully utilized to bring an actor to the height of his ability.

Jac Lewis

PART I:
THE ROLE
OF THE COSTUME

-visual is where Ana Diosdado +
Concha Romero prepare Pilar +
distance selves from audience

Chapter 1
THE INSPIRATION

> "Cost they habit as thy purse can buy,
> But not express'd in fancy; rich, not gaudy,
> For the apparel oft proclaims the man."
> *Polonium, in "Hamlet"*

As a respectful son, Laertes listened carefully to his father's advice. It is possible that Laertes already knew the valuable impression clothing imparts and its influence upon the reaction of onlookers. The effect of attire upon the wearer, as well as the observer, is a realization that comes early in life.

The favorite fantasy of childhood is to be grown-up, and instinctively we know that the only way we can feel the part is by dressing for it with the inspiration provided by clothing we do not usually wear. So Mother's dress, hat and high-heeled shoes become our first costume, allowing us to enter the world of imagination and enabling us to play a role we would not effectively create without the costume. To the imaginative child, wearing someone else's garments is the first inspirational step toward the development of a new identity; the first opportunity to place himself in the skin of another person; his first acting role.

The Importance of Apparel on Moods

The game of dressing up teaches us the importance of apparel upon our own moods, the message we wish to convey to others, the suitability of clothing to our varying activities. In everyday life people dress to fulfill their subconscious vision of themselves. The effect of clothes upon one's psychological outlook is unlimited: the stance and manner of an athlete can be assumed by wearing a pair of jogging shoes and a sweatsuit; a well-tailored suit reinforces a businessman or woman; a handsomely cut tuxedo establishes an air of sophistication; a flowing chiffon gown allows a woman to feel ethereal and elegant. In our personal lives we play many roles, and dress to befit the occasion.

Play-acting, aided by costuming, is part of our natural way

of living; every day, depending upon our chosen activity, we dress and act the part. The clothing not only presents a person judged by others, but the person we feel ourselves to be. Our garb affects the aspect we have of ourselves, while indicating to others the role we have undertaken to publicly express. How many times have we said, while dressing in garments that enhance our appearance: "I feel like a new person"? Our whole being seems to change; with spirits lifted, our facial expression alters. Even a new color affects our attitude and emotion.

As an actor, you, in your varying roles, indeed become a new person. It is the physical change which the actor must undergo to accomplish the desired effect, and that material alteration is produced by the costume. Thereupon the actor becomes another individual prior to his speaking a line, for he reacts to the effect of his character's dress instantly, even before he steps onto the stage. The wardrobe *performs* along with the spoken word. The physical change, established by the clothing, make-up and accessories, helps the performer *maintain* the new mental attitude each part demands.

The theatre is called a magical place of make-believe, and sorcery is evoked when an actor dons a costume that transforms him into someone else. If it is a period costume, he is transplanted back in time. The actor, in essence, is a magician, creating an illusion which the audience accepts to be true.

John Gielgud

John Gielgud had never performed in the United States until 1928, when he was unexpectedly summoned to New York by Leslie Faber, his actor-friend who was preparing to appear there in Alfred Neumann's *The Patriot*. The purpose of the summons was for him to join Faber in the cast as a last-minute replacement of an inadequate performer in the role of Tsarevitch Alexander. When Gielgud sailed from England, he spent his time aboard ship studying the script which had been sent to him. It was urgent to be fully prepared since he was forewarned that the play was opening immediately upon his arrival and there would be time for him to participate in only one rehearsal before the opening performance. Although he had but a few short scenes, it was exciting to Gielgud to be appearing in New York. Nevertheless it was alarming to have so limited a time for rehearsal.

However, his apprehension was soon assuaged when he discovered waiting for him a costume which he regarded as superb. He was provided with a handsome wig of powered chestnut-colored hair, and a splendid cloak with an ermine cape. As he put it on, he felt so magnificent, he was certain he would be a dashing figure. The costume gave Gielgud tremendous support and inspired his confidence.

The clothing, hair style and accessories are the fuel which feeds the acting machinery and makes it work. A musician has his instrument to use to interpret a composer's music. The actor's instrument is his body, and the costume becomes part of his body in movement, mood and time. The costume is more than an accessory. From the beginning of learning a part, the importance of its fluence on the ultimate importance must be understood.

Michael Redgrave said: "The summit of an actor's art is to make us forget he is an actor." His costume helps him forget he is an actor, and aids him in becoming the person he is portraying. The character's garments do not serve just to mask the performer, but reflect the character, his life style, habits, background and breeding. ✳

Costumes Must be Believable

A costume must be believable and the actor must believe in it as though it were part of his personal wardrobe. He must like the wardrobe, and admire it to the extent that he knows instinctively it is right for him in the part he is playing. He must feel satisfied in the clothes even when the script calls for a character to look run-down and miserable. The actor will absorb the force of his attire and react accordingly. He is not just "spending a holiday" in his costume. In effect, he is living in it permanently.

I Pagliacci

In Ruggiero Leoncavallo's opera *I Pagliacci*, the actor Canio rightfully suspects a love affair between his wife Nedda and Silvio, all members of a traveling-actors troupe. Canio, dressed and made up as the clown Pagliacci in this play-within-a-play, portrays a man betrayed by his wife Columbine and her lover Harlequin, performed by Nedda and Silvio. Canio becomes so immersed in his role of the deceived Punchinello, he cannot distinguish between reality and acting. Neither can the spectators. Not able to separate the performance from actuality, they believe Canio's stabbing of Nedda to be part of the play. It is not until he removes Pagliacci's clown hat and declares to the audience: "No Punchinello am I, but a man," do they grasp the truth. The spell that is cast when an actor dons a costume is awesome. The transformation is a mystical event.

Nijinsky

In his normal everyday appearance, Nijinsky was a squat, not particularly graceful individual. In his *Petrouchka* costume he became the limply graceful puppet. When he danced *Spectre de la Rose*, the delicacy of the costume, working its own wonders, transformed him into the fragile flower.

Costumes Create a Mood

The costume establishes an *atmosphere* blending with the scenery. This atmosphere permeates and sets the mood, time and place. Costumes are as important to each scene as living, breathing people. Even on a bare stage the costume reveals the aura of the period.

Small details, often taken for granted, play a very important role. A frill, a ruffle, a trimming used correctly, can elicit a response that otherwise would not be there, thus enriching an actor's performance. The very touch and sight of the texture and color of the costume will summon a stimulation he may not have previously experienced. Imagine the sensation velvet, silk, or brocade might evoke in you, as opposed to your reaction to the prickliness of rough cloth or straw.

Costumes for Disguises

To create a disguise the costume is an absolute necessity. Shakespeare used all the jugglery of disguises and recognitions which were reliant upon the costume. Boys played women in Shakespeare's theatre and were entirely dependent upon correct dress to create the illusion of femininity. A boy playing the role of Juliet was influenced by his attire in order for him to accept himself as a young girl. He had to handle it with proficiency so as not to destroy the illusion and become an unintended buffoon.

Until the early 1930s in the universities of England, theatrical performances were given solely by male students who performed the necessary female roles. They had to first disguise themselves as women, and then proceed to perform the part. Therefore, at any time on stages where women were not part of the cast, the costume became a disguise within a disguise. Acting is the ability to persuade the audience that this is the true character, and the actor, through the costume, is persuading himself that he is the character. Thus the actor is disguising his own personality.

Boy as Shakespearean actor in sixteenth-century male and female costumes.

Where does the actor begin to learn how to interpret his role? Of course lines are learned first. But to put life into them with passion, manner and posture, requires research into the character portrayed. The script and costume share an equal importance since they both present the essence of the role, and work together with the actor to develop the part. The purpose of the play is to tell a visual story, and the actor uses his own imagination as to the sensibility and responsive actions of the person depicted.

How does one arrive at such emotions? Only by getting into the skin of the individual, and the clothing of the character is the outer skin.

When John Gielgud acquired the part of the king in Gordon Daviot's *Richard of Bordeaux* he was delighted with it since he felt it was suitable to his own personality and mannerisms. His assurance was further enhanced when he discovered that his costumes inspired him to exactly express the development of Richard's character and his gradual aging.

To be an inspired actor is to perform an act of transfiguration. Ultimately make-up and costume are not disguises, but formations of another being. If you choose not to make yourself unrecognizable as another person and you are relying upon your own outer appearance and mannerisms, you are only giving a surface portrayal and being yourself acting a part. Your own physical attributes may not be enough.

Chapter 2
RESEARCH

Now that you have the idea of what your role will require in the way of a costume, and yet you realize that you will not receive that costume until dress parade and rehearsal, how are you going to develop the character's movements, posture and feeling without the costume?

The answer is: research, improvisation, and experiments, all accomplished in many ways.

Rip Torn

Rip Torn enjoys being a character actor because it expands his knowledge and is a vehicle for constant study and discovery. A change of type of role is an experience he regards as a method of keeping acting fresh and exciting. In his search as to how an individual would behave, move and talk in a given period, he adopts the attitude of a detective.

Total Research Required

A dedicated actor is studious about his role. He researches the exact years in which his character lived, concentrating upon the mores, history and clothing of the time. He does not limit his research to an ethnic accent of the people of a particular country or area; he investigates the manner in which they walked, sat and stood in the clothes of that period and place; he discovers the accessories to their apparel and the fashion in which they were used. He reads as much detail as possible about the background of the character he is to portray, he delves into behavior, dress and habits. He is then able to complete a biographical probe and construct the nature of the character.

Gather facts regarding the architecture of the period, and the furnishings of the households, so that you may understand the restrictions certain types of chairs and sofas might impose. You would then be able to imagine what they required of the posture of the people of that era in order to sit upon them and the manner in which wearing apparel had to be arranged when they were seated.

13

Combined with your newly acquired knowledge of how people appeared and your concentration upon the fabrics of their garments — whether of homespun cloth or luxurious satins and velvets — your emotional response to the costume you will be wearing becomes enhanced. Some of the clothing of certain periods was constructed with heavy fabrics. Your study will enable you to anticipate the weight of your particular costume and the influence that weight will have upon your movement and performance.

Elizabeth the Queen

In Maxwell Anderson's play *Elizabeth the Queen*, the final scene is the confrontation of Elizabeth with Lord Essex just before he is to be executed. The Queen is laden with many sorrows, for not only is she old and weary, but she has made the terrible decision of death for the man she loves. When Lynn Fontanne portrayed Elizabeth, she wore a cloth-of-gold gown that weighed at least twenty-five pounds, and although it was a burden to wear, it aided her to portray, both physically and emotionally, the weight of her years and frightful decision. Beverly Sills, singing the role of Elizabeth in Gaetano Donizetti's opera *Roberto Devereaux*, wore an even heavier costume, and it, too, heightened her dramatic performance and helped her reveal the onerous responsibilities of the Queen.

The political and social times in which your character lived — its poetry, music and literature — are all essential parts of your knowledge since dress, posture and mannerisms were influenced by them. Research them the way you research the character, and you will become a genuine figure of that time in history to which you completely belong.

Dance and the Costume

Dance is also a reflection of the era since clothing and dance are integrated in a special manner. It would be impossible to convey the graceful, studied movements of the gavotte or minuet in anything but the costume of the period, for it was that peculiar kind of restraint which the clothing dictated that created the movements of those dances. The abandonment and freedom in dancing the jitterbug of the 1940s was identified by the short, swinging skirt. Each variety of dance is exacted in movement by the attire of the dancers. Observation will reveal to you the manner of dance movement in conjunction with the use of your costume.

COPYRIGHT ©BETH BERGMAN 1990

Beverly Sills as Queen Elizabeth in Donizetti's Roberto Devereaux.

Sources for Research

Museums. If you are appearing in a period or classic play, study the portraits of the particular time. Note the manner in which the people sit and stand. When women wore corsets, their bodies were held rigidly, and sat in stiff, upright positions. Since body movements were limited when they walked, gracefulness was conveyed mainly through the use of arms and head, and with accessories such as gloves, fans, parasols and hats. Pay close attention to the manner in which women used these accessories. Not only is the basic costume tantamount to the visual and inner aspect of a character, but so are the costume's accessories, and these accessories will aid you in forming the character and developing a style. Consider how much can be revealed through the use of a fan: dismay, shyness, coyness, flirtatiousness, a commanding gesture — all dependant upon the temperament of the character and the situation occurring in the play.

Libraries. Read as much as you can on the history, biographies and customs of the time. Examine books of paintings and photographs of the past, noting clothing and their predominating colors, and jewelry used for adornment, so that in being acquainted with them your feeling for the era is intensified. Find issues of old magazines and newspapers and observe how people dressed and posed.

Movies and Television. Movies are the visual source of record we have today of both the actual and reconstructed past, enabling an actor to study movement of dress and manner of posture. There are occasions when a degree of authenticity is lacking in historical movie costuming, or modern touches are allowed to creep in. However, there are many fine motion pictures, particularly British films and television productions, that give exact and representative historical costuming. These films, with their costumes, lighting and photography, depict the flavor of the times. Watch old movies which appear on television to observe actors and actresses moving and posturing in various costumes, including period and modern clothes. You'll learn from them.

Clothing as a Clue to Character

The role is yours. You have memorized your lines; you understand the person you are enacting: his thoughts, his motivations. But there are certain aspects that you have not yet captured. First, how does he appear to others? Since clothing describes the man, so it is through your costume you first introduce him to the audience. Next, although you understand his nature, how can you know his feelings at that stage in his life you are reproducing? You must send two messages at the same time: One is to deliver a portrait to the audience; two, is for you to convey the character's emotions. Whether you approach character development from the outside in, or the inside out, you are nevertheless reliant upon your costume to form the complete picture.

Clothing is a clue to the attitude of people since it always reflects the sentiment of the time in which they lived. More freedom in the clothing has been the aftermath of wars, since peacetime releases restrictions. Following the French Revolution there was an attempt to return to the classic loose-fitting Grecian clothes for women and away from the tight-fitting clothing of the aristocratic French courts. After the First World War women's skirts became shorter and, as time passes, increased freedom of spirit is represented by the great latitudes in current fashion.

Just the way you develop the individual you are personifying and his situation in relation to the other characters in the play, so you must put as much concern into researching your costume completely. In order to fully discover all the facets of the person you are portraying, be a sleuth on the prowl.

Let us assume you are an actress who has acquired the role of a flapper from the Twenties. There are abundant sources for your research, improvisations, and experiments. In the library you will dig out magazines and newspapers of the 1920s and observe

17

in old photographs how the flapper is dressed, the way she poses with her hands, feet and head. Study her accessories: hat, shoes, long beads, rolled stockings, hair styles.

Improvise

Improvise parts of clothing, and act in them. Wear a short dress, put on long beads, roll your stockings, chew gum. In a thrift shop, find a cloche hat. Experiment with your accessories: take gloves off, put them on, play with the beads. Learn to dance the Charleston. Watch old movies.

The thrift shop should not be overlooked as a valuable resource for a glimpse into the past in addition to being a wonderful, inexpensive source of costume for you while you are building your character.

Alfred Lunt

The dedicated actor is concerned about what he will wear in a play. When Alfred Lunt was portraying Captain Bluntschli in George Bernard Shaw's *Arms and the Man*, he carefully noted the playwright's description of this Revolutionary War soldier as "in a deplorable plight, bespattered with mud and snow." He went to great pains to dampen his soldier's uniform, bring it up to the roof of his Lexington Avenue apartment building and hang the uniform on a clothes line. The costume was rained on, sun-bleached, suffered all the hazards of outdoor exposure, and was periodically subjected to a rug beater in the hands of the actor. Then, to provide the ultimate touch, he took a needle to his thumb to draw blood with which to provide a further instance of torture to the uniform and the soldier. Alfred Lunt had the insight to know that he as well as the audience would *believe* he had been through much ordeal even before he appeared on stage.

If an actor's fame and reputation survive even beyond his life, there is always a good reason for it. Most often it is due to his own demands upon himself for perfection. Certain actors are referred to repeatedly as models of devotion to every facet of acting. If again and again, reference is made to their manner of exploring the roles undertaken by them, it is to suggest to you that their particular paths are well worth following.

18

Julie Harris

It is neither accident nor good fortune that brought to Julie Harris the unprecedented distinction of being the only person to receive five Antoinette Perry awards for her Broadway performances. Woven between those particular roles, for which she will always be remembered with a special sense of awe, are so many diversified characters she has assumed both on stage and in film that it would be literally impossible to enumerate them individually. Her first distinguishing part was the adolescent Frankie in Carson McCullers' *The Member of the Wedding*, and afterwards she gathered Tony awards like flowers for characterizations uniquely and indelibly conceived. To have the ability to range from the courageous Joan of Arc in *The Lark*, the reckless Sally in *I Am a Camera*, the independent divorcee of *Forty Carats*, the bereaved and maligned Mrs. Lincoln, to the insightful, sensitive Emily Dickinson: *The Belle of Amherst*, indicates an actress who combines her innate acting talent with an inquisitiveness that leads her to every avenue of means for a full understanding and interpretation of her myriad roles.

To depict a historical figure offers exacting and exciting possibilities to an actor. It is an undertaking ambiguously easy and difficult. Easy, because there is much available information in the annuls of literature and history; difficult, because the person is well known, placing the interpretation under particular scrutiny by the audience. Absolutely authentic research is then demanded.

Appearing in Jean Anouilh's *The Lark*, Julie Harris created a living Joan of Arc. In search of the true Joan, she reached as far back as the actual records of the court trial, studying them so as to bring an authentic St. Joan into existence. Julie Harris's portrayal of Mary Todd Lincoln was equally realistic because she steeped herself in the events and circumstances of Mrs. Lincoln's life. And although these two completely unlike historical figures were represented by the same actress, in each unique performance the actress's individuality was completely submerged.

Costume Characterization in Amadeus

In the London production of Peter Shaffer's *Amadeus*, Paul Scofield as Solieri, and Simon Callow as Mozart, were presented with the identical situation. Shaffer's lines were descriptive of Mozart's character, and Callow felt that he could rely upon them to evoke the kind of fellow his rival Solieri could learn to hate. At the same time he was to show the playfulness and genius of the composer, and ultimately to evoke compassion for this complex young man. Through many rehearsals, Callow could not find the way through delineating all these facets.

To begin to understand Mozart, it is necessary to be aware of his physical shortcomings. He had a large head on a small body, a huge nose and an overlapping upper lip, all contributing toward making him unattractive, except for his abundant blond hair. As he grew older, he learned to overcome his imperfections by splendid dress of lace-trimmed shirts, blue square-cut coat and gold buttons, knee breeches and silver-buckled shoes. Mozart knew the importance of costume for one's own feeling of enhancement.

But for Callow this key to Mozart was not known to him, and it was only when he discovered a useful biography did he encounter the core of Mozart. A richness of description can fire the development of a character for the actor in search of the truth.

Details Shape Great Performances

A creative actor continually searches for new ways to improve and refine his work. Julie Harris is firmly identified with her effective conception of Emily Dickinson in William Luce's one-character play, *The Belle of Amherst*, and it is a role she is continually invited to re-create. She has so become at one with Emily Dickinson it may be taken for granted that she has "frozen" the part; nevertheless, she continually probes for discoveries. When Julie Harris made still another pilgrimage to Emily Dickinson's home in Amherst, she found a dress hanging behind the poet's bedroom door. She had the dress duplicated, and together with the addition of some recently uncovered poems, added a new dimension and enthusiasm to her portrayal.

Nothing is too miniscule in researching a character. During Alfred Lunt's preparation for his role in *The Visit* by Friedrich Dürrenmatt, he picked up two pebbles in Central Park, deciding that he would shake them out of his shoe as a bit of appropriate stage business. During rehearsal he sought out the advice of Peter

Brook, who directed the play, as to whether he thought it might be better if he used only one pebble. Scrupulous attention to small details shapes great performances.

Alfred Lunt and Lynn Fontanne had built a reputation for extraordinary research in their passion for perfection. Their first Theatre Guild play was *The Guardsman*, and playwright Ferenc Molnár's characters were a married Hungarian actor and actress. The husband challenged his wife's faithfulness by using his acting abilities to assume the identity of an officer of the Russian Guard intent upon pursuing her. The Lunts decided that they could never be convincingly Hungarian if they didn't go to Hungary. So they withdrew money from her bank account and off they went to Budapest, where they encountered a Russian who had been an officer in the czar's army, and who was now a doorman. Alfred Lunt drew a sketch of his uniform, which he had duplicated when the Lunts went on to London. To have the proper military de-meanor demanded when he was disguised as the Russian officer, Lunt had his head shaved, knowing that when he was on stage as the actor-husband, he would wear a wig. Lynn Fontanne, on her part, bought a thousand dollar white evening gown in Paris which she felt necessary to be sufficiently alluring for intrigue. They came back home with no money except for cab fare to their apartment, but satisfied that they had completely explored their characters.

No one is asking you to go to such lengths. But it does point out the fact that all of these actors drew no limits in their prepara-tory research for the essence in a role. An actor should be scrupu-lous in every detail to create a character.

Chapter 3
ACCESSORIES

The accessories of a costume are a valuable asset to an actor's performance, and it is incumbent upon the actor to learn to use accessories long before the dress rehearsal has bestowed them upon him. A substitute is easily obtainable beforehand from the wardrobe department, a thrift shop, or among your own possessions, and the importance of collaboration with them to enhance a performance is inestimable.

In preparing your role, it is necessary to improvise and use your costume at the same time you are learning your lines. In lieu of the actual costume during the course of your preparation, we will now turn to the use of accessories as a substitute. Some of these accessories will also be part of your permanent costume, and you will acquaint yourself with the integral part they will play in your interpretation as they are applied in a variety of manners to convey mood, character and action.

Effective Use of Seemingly Insignificant Objects

A handkerchief, which might be considered an insignificant object, has the power to strike a tremendous effect. In a period play it flutters in the hands of an ingenue. A tragedienne, in a heartrending drama, wrings her handkerchief and weeps into it. Tucked into the breast pocket of a suit jacket, it announces a well-turned-out gentleman. A red and blue printed cotton handkerchief tied around the neck of an actor will turn him into a cowboy; with the same handkerchief tied around his nose and lower part of his face, the same actor becomes a thief or bandit.

Shakespeare's *Othello* has a handkerchief as its center of tragedy, and Laurence Olivier originated an untraditional response in the handkerchief scene with Iago. Instead of the customary action of whipping Iago's face with the handkerchief, Olivier chose to stroke his face gently with it, as if to suggest that Iago could not be making a serious suggestion of an unfaithful Desdemona. With a slight change in gesture with the same small handkerchief, an entirely different idea is conveyed.

Some performers have paired their careers with an identifying prop or accessory, including the handkerchief. In the 1930s, musical comedy and nightclub singer Sophie Tucker made a chiffon handkerchief her trademark. And can you imagine Louis Armstrong without his handkerchief? Although not an actor, he knew that with it he established an image that became his identity. Luciano Pavarotti, as an opera singer in concert, clings to his handkerchief and binds an audience to himself.

Accessories Help to Create Character

Whatever the accessory, it can be applied in infinite ways for infinite effects. The cane or walking stick is used to great advantage in expressing a broad range of meaning, depending upon how it is manipulated. It can tell an audience that a character is an old, feeble person. The cane can suggest a debonair gentleman and in a subtle change of handling it, the cane becomes the property of a fop or dandy. The cane yields so many marvelous effects in dance and vaudeville dancers can hardly do without them; in their soft-shoe numbers, canes and straw hats are permanent partners. Charlie Chaplin's cane helped to give birth to his famous tramp; and his adroit use of it conveyed a myriad of emotions and situations.

The accessory speaks in its own peculiar way. A metal badge says "I am an officer of the law — a sheriff or a policeman." Before the actor utters a line, he feels and the audience knows

Vaudeville man with cane.

his status. The vest is another example of an accessory capable of establishing individuality. Put one on and you will appear and feel important, for a vest is an authoritarian symbol. Small accessory — large impression.

Collars and Neckties

Something as simple as a collar will convey a wealth of information. The small white Peter Pan collar (which was often identified with Claudette Colbert in the films) suggests youth, innocence and demureness. It is used many times in courtroom scenes of murder melodramas to indicate the innocence of the defendant. Just the manner in which the collar is upturned produces many effects. Half-turned up, it can imply hasty, careless dressing. Turned all the way up, it can present a range of situations from poverty to attempted disguise. A woman in an upturned collar is regal and elegant; if it's a fur collar, she exemplifies opulance, luxury and wealth. A man in a stiff collar is a figure of control; it establishes a businessman's commanding competence. The hard reversed collar of the priest summons respect. The firm collars of both men indicate prestige. The shape and fabric of the collar establishes the attitude of an era: the lacy, frilled collar was the fashion of a frivolous age; the flat, white broad collar belonged to the austere Puritan. They are all at your disposal to serve as easy-to-use building blocks for characterization.

Think of what you can do with just a necktie or any of its variations. Properly and carefully knotted, loosened or untied, you have an inkling of the man and his circumstances. A jabot for the courtier, or an ascot for the gentleman who rides the hounds — whatever you have placed around your neck has helped make you become whoever you choose to be. In conjunction with the dialogue you are learning, the accessories become part of the art of interpretation.

Many Uses of the Shawl

Among the easily obtainable accessories is the shawl. It is an extremely valuable item since it affords a tremendous scope of application. Ruth Draper, the renowned monologist, was a mistress of the use of the shawl and with it she conveyed an affecting range of expression and mood. As a wrapping for an infant, it arouses a sense of comfort, warmth and tenderness; a shawl covering the head of a woman holding the infant endows her with the aura of a Madonna; around the shoulders of an old person it discloses feebleness or illness. The shawl is the expression of a grand scale of emotions: placed over the head it will cast a spell of either sorrow or furtiveness, depending upon the body's movement; an appropriate gesture with a shawl invokes a sense of utter hopelessness, and the Greek tragedies cannot be separated from the use of the shawl for the translation of gestures into overwhelming grief. Covering a portion of the face and revealing only the eyes, it can be alluring and flirtatious. It becomes part of a gypsy's free, unfettered movements.

In Henrik Ibsen's *The Doll's House*, Nora is to dance the tarantella at a party, and her husband bids her to rehearse the dance before him. It is at a time when she feels trapped by her circumstances, and her emotions are in direct opposition to the abandonment the tarantella demands. The shawl is an integral part of the dance, and an actress who portrays Nora has an opportunity to foreshadow, with the use of the shawl, the freedom Nora begins to experience in the dance and her ultimate choice of a life without binding restrictions. The use of a simple accessory can become an affecting device. Actresses who understand and appreciate the potentialities of the shawl and acquire skills in handling it have embraced a potent tool.

Use of a Cape

The cape is as expressive as the shawl in the definition of character and emotion. An actor portraying a man of royalty strives to demonstrate his might. With postured flourish of the cape he can express all-encompassing power; if he is a tyrannical ruler, he can reveal his meanness and cruelty through regal and austere display of that cape. Visualize a deposed king, deprived of his power, crumpled, crushed, sitting hunched over on his throne, his cape cast before him, revealing utter defeat. As a stealthy disguise the cape takes on an aura of concealment, its inner pockets a possible hiding place for weapons or stolen property. It may be brandished in a flamboyant and nonchalant manner. Used appropriately, it speaks lines along with your own.

26

Expressive Use of Fans

Aside from its advantages for flirting, the fan is still another item capable of lending a variety of expressions. Open or closed, with an either rapid or slow twist of the wrist, it is capable of imparting a scale of attitudes from excitement to cool self-confidence. It comes in as many shapes, forms and types as there are possibilities for application. The small lace fan that was fashionable in the mid-nineteeth century presents a vastly different picture and use than the large ostrich or peacock feathered fans of the Egyptian courts.

In many countries the fan had been a popular accessory for both men and women, and its purposes were abundant and diversified. Although its original purpose was to stir life into warm, heavy air, it developed a life of its own. Secrets were whispered behind the fans of gossips, courtiers and connivers, and many an intrigue was fostered behind a fan. It became the sweet, charming allurement of a maiden. It was vigorously shaken in outrage and anger. It was pointed and thrust as a gesture of authority. As a disguise and cover-up, it had found still another purpose. It could be used regally or with coquettry.

It takes practice and talent to maneuver a fan correctly. When Florenz Ziegfeld adorned his statuesque show girls with huge fans as headdresses, it took plenty of work to learn the trick of balancing them while walking down winding staircases, and at the same time remembering to look beautiful and smile.

In the 1930s, just the right flip of a fan brought fame to a girl in Chicago. At the city's world's fair, known as the Century of Progress, despite all of the exhibits of science's latest advances, it was Sally Rand and her fan dance who made history. It was rumored that all Sally wore was her two fans, and her manipulative peek-a-boo with them was enough progress for anybody.

An actor has his accessories and his choices.

Eyeglasses Suggest Character Types

Consider the multitude of types of people you can produce with an ordinary accessory: eyeglasses. The business executive's authority, the banker's dignity, the lawyer's knowledge — all appear to be confirmed by the fact they are wearing eyeglasses, mysteriously endowing them with an air of dependability. The more adventuresome traits are identified by the aviator's glasses and the motorcyclist's or skier's goggles. While dark glasses and a cane may indicate a blind individual, the very shape of a pair of sunglasses can render a person either practical or fashionable. The spectacles favored by the scholar, academic or accountant marks the position in a career; half-glasses worn by grandparents and their contemporaries signal a stage of life. For each type of glasses you choose to wear, you almost automatically become a particular sort of person.

Glasses typify eras and attitudes. The lorgnette of the 1700s was useful in observing others either in disdainful regard or prying curiosity. The monocle of the eighteenth century and Edwardian period became the affectation of a mannered gentleman. Wearing a monocle was an accomplishment in itself, which you will discover if you are called upon to wear one. It's not a simple matter to nestle a single lens over one eye, and only practice makes it possible.

The mousy, unattractive girl unnoticed by the handsome man whom she loved was a classic situation in the old movies. Her round, steel-rimmed, prim-and-prissy glasses were eventually tenderly removed by the hero while he exclaimed: "Why, Miss Jones, you're beautiful!" A backward look at old movie classics and eyeglasses recalls the silent film actor Harold Lloyd, whose famed trademark was his horn-rimmed glasses. With them he became a lovable, naïve nitwit.

In calculating the variety of eyeglasses in existence — from frameless to horn-rimmed to harlequin-shaped — you can see before you as many identifiable personalities and possibilities. When a play spans many years and the character passes from youth to advanced years, eyeglasses are often worn to quickly indicate the aging process. In addition to describing a character, eyeglasses held or moved in an actor's hands can enable him to express, along with his words, a state of emotion. While you are home learning your lines, this simple accessory can help you to become acquainted with the character you are evolving.

Shoes Reveal Character

When an unidentified American Indian stated that to know

28

what a man is like you must be in his shoes, he hit upon a basic truth for the actor. Need and fashion dictate various styles, shapes and forms of shoes and each type of shoe influences the actor's posture and walk.

The Western cowboy in his boots is compelled to walk differently than the businessman wearing his highly polished wing tips. A young woman running along in her jogging shoes isn't going to be able to run the same way in a pair of high-heeled pumps. Walk, posture and attitude immediately change with the alteration of the style of shoe. No one is inclined to take vigorous strides in high-heeled sandals; on the other hand, riding boots do not encourage dainty steps. A military man's entire bearing and demeanor is influenced by his heavy Army boots. A dancing shoe calls out for litheness; a pair of sturdy flat shoes demands a heavy, firm walk.

Dirk Bogarde is of the opinion that the most essential part of the wardrobe is shoes. He discovered that while wearing them he can find the identifying walk of the person he his playing; from that acquired walk naturally follows the carriage. Shoes dictate the bearing of shoulders, encouraging them to be straight, or compelling them to sag or hunch. As with shoulders, the neck is affected as well, becoming erect or slanted to the side.

Each person has an individual walk and posture, and the type of shoe he regularly wears affects it. Put on tight or uncomfortable shoes, and then observe your face and posture in the mirror. Wear a pair of shoes that squeak, and notice how your walk echoes that squeak. The frame of the body becomes shaped by the shoes. Wearing shoes that alter your walk and posture, together with clothing appropriate to the role you are undertaking, another human form — no longer your own familiar shape — is created. Mae West appeared to be tall and voluptuous but in fact was a short woman. She established the illusion of height and adopted a sensuous walk by wearing high-heeled platform shoes underneath her long gowns.

During a trip to Russia, Joshua Logan attended a rehearsal of Modest Moussorgsky's opera, *Boris Godunov*, which Stanislavski was directing. Logan thought the young man portraying Boris was uninteresting and colorless. But in performance, thanks to elevated shoes, the singer was six inches taller. Along with a majestic wig and eyes enhanced by dark make-up, he became every inch a towering, powerful czar.

As soon as possible, it is important to wear the style of shoe called for in your development of the person you are striving to bring into being. You must become accustomed to them since his essential posture is an important key. It is not easy to be comfortable and walk naturally in a shoe which is new to you. While Robert Donat was filming his famous *Goodbye, Mr. Chips*, even when away from the set, he wore Mr. Chipping's shoes in order to keep the character within himself, and not to lose sight of him.

Alfred Lunt used shoes as an acting aid in an entirely original fashion as Captain Bluntschli in Shaw's *Arms and the Man*. Although immediately upon his first entrance, through his methodical seasoning and conditioning of the soldier's uniform, he conveyed to himself and the audience that he had experienced horrendous times, he also had to convincingly express the utter exhaustion of his body. On reflecting how he could accomplish this, he dismissed the possibility of actually putting himself in a condition of extreme fatigue beforehand since it would not only be wearing upon him physically to do so performance after performance, it would also present the difficulty of then having to be energetic throughout the remainder of the play.

Once again his ingenuity and thoroughness solved the dilemma. He wore a pair of light leather boots; into their soles he inserted thinly sliced pieces of lead. The lead in his boots made walking a tiring business, and when the action called for him to fall upon a bed, with those heavily weighted feet dangling over its edge, he was one worn-out soldier. It was his own secret device, knowing when it was necessary to put the lead in — and when to get the lead out.

With shoes it naturally follows to consider hosiery. A sheer pair of nylons will certainly produce in you a feeling quite apart from what you would experience if you were wearing white cotton stockings. Suppose a character wears short socks with high-heeled shoes? Or black lace stockings along with a jogging shoe? Each style of shoe combined with a particular type of hosiery indicates a specific character designation, from elegant to comic.

Gloves Exemplify Types

Your personal rehearsal aids in the form of accessories are almost without limit. A glove is able to convey what a bare hand cannot. Gloves exemplify the type of person you are going to portray and their varieties range from long, white, elegant formal gloves worn at the dance to baseball gloves. The construction worker, the coal miner, the ditch digger, each has his own kind of glove and his movements are influenced with their use. The chef has his glove, the Eskimo his, and so does the skier. There are mittens and little lace gloves; the gloves of a courtier as he sweeps them in a deep bow, and the gauntlet glove of the knight. Each pair of hands, in a pair of gloves of a particular sort, moves in its own way; when removed from the hands, the glove demands a special manner of being held. Just as the movements of bare hands are expressive, so is the message cloaked with meaning when delivered with the glove. It is an accessory with a great deal to indicate, and another aid in your delineation. And while we are discussing hands and gloves, let's not overlook polished fingernails and their individual effect if the shade is a delicate pale pink or a dragonlady ruby red.

The Importance of Jewelry

In 1919, when Ruth Gordon was chosen to play in Booth Tarkington's *Seventeen*, she was given money to buy her own stage wardrobe since she strongly voiced her opinion that the costume was part of her performance. She put equal emphasis upon the importance of jewelry, and looked back upon her costume and jewelry in *Ethan Frome* with particular tenderness. Recalling that it was her character's best dress, what made it feel very special was the blue enamel locket worn on a thin gold chain. Later, when Ruth Gordon heard that Guthrie McClintic was about to do a play for which she wanted to audition, her first thoughts concerned her uncertainty as to how to dress for it and if any of her jewelry would be appropriate.

Jewelry is an additional and important accessory, as every woman knows. A simple gold locket on a fine chain around her neck affects her in a manner quite apart from the moment when an emerald necklace caresses her throat. Gold hoop earrings can produce a seductive air, and long diamond earrings dropping from her earlobes will turn her into a woman of mannered elegance. A man secures a stickpin into his necktie, and he assumes a suave appearance. If it's a diamond horseshoe stickpin he inserts into a stock tie, he experiences the sense of an affluent man of the turn of the century. Add a pair of cuff links and his urbane demeanor seems to increase.

Jewelry can be one of your best friends as you construct your role.

The Many Uses of Hats

Hats top off the costume, and they disclose as many facts as there are types of hats. They reveal one's age, profession, social position, activity, formality or casualness. History can be written with hats alone, and they suggest the prevading attitudes of successive periods. The steeple-whimple ladies' headdress was borne with the dignity of the Middle Ages; the plain bonnet of the year 1800 reflected the demure life of the period. The lavishness of the Gay Nineties was illustrated by magnificently flowered and feathered hats worn by the ladies and the top hats of their escorts. A cap was the possession of a hardworking laborer. The wars of the world introduced military hats ranging from feathers and plumage to steel helmets. While sailing the ocean blue in wartime as well as peacetime, hats announce the rank of the admiral, the captain of the ship or the sailor. The yachting cap belongs to the wealthy gentleman and a more utilitarian hat protects the commercial fisherman as he weathers storms.

The hat represents more than the era and station in life. The very way it is worn or handled is a further revelation. A man's straw or felt hat worn in conventional manner indicates a conventional person; the same hat tilted upward and pushed back signals casual behavior; a hat precariously perched on the head

32

could signify that he is drunk; if he slouches it downward over his face, he's probably trying to make himself appear inconspicuous. A hat in the hand will imply a shy, insecure person, or a humble and deprecating demeanor — or simply a polite gesture. A courtier removes his plumed hat and displays grace and courtesy with a touch of royalty. A hat can disclose a menacing and evil person. It can be an extension of one's thoughts as well as inner nature.

For Maurice Evans, hats were the tip-off to the development of his understanding of Richard II when he played the role in an Old Vic production. He had a short time in which to prepare, and a remark made by the costume designer David Ffoulkes gave him a clue to the volatile Richard. Ffoulkes believed it was ridiculous for Richard to constantly wear a crown just because he was a king, for it is unreasonable to assume that kings go around all day and sleep at night with crowns upon their heads.

Therefore, to match Richard's youth, for the early part of the play the designer created a range of debonair, jewel-encrusted hats, with colorful Italian-style costumes. Underneath those impudent hats Evans found a willful lad. The metamorphosis of the high-spirited young king into a man forged by misfortune created a deeply moving moment when Evans wore a crown for the first time only to surrender it to Bolinbroke, with the line "Here, cousin, seize the crown," exhibiting Richard's love of the dramatic touch. Evolving from hats to crown, Evans drew out the qualities of the king.

For you hats can be a challenge. In our hatless society, once you put on any kind of hat you're in for a surprise. If you have to balance a "Merry Widow" hat on your head, you've a great deal of conditioning ahead of you to learn to hold your head up high and your back erect. Suddenly you experience a flood of understanding of how people felt and acted towards one another. Immediately you will be elegant and proud — that is, if the hat doesn't fall off your head. By becoming familiar with the use of hats, you have a valuable additional approach to your understanding a personality.

Barnard Hughes and his wife appeared together in *Anniversary Waltz* which he regarded as a very simple comedy requiring little effort. He had recently bought the type of tweed hat associated with Rex Harrison and, on the spur of the moment, he decided to wear it the opening night of the play. Suddenly and unexpectedly, the character re-emerged for him with an entirely new presence. By taking his hat off and tossing it up and down, and generally fussing with the crease of the hat, he closed gaps in the part of which he had never before been aware.

There is a proper hat and a proper wearing and handling of it for every occasion. A hat, in a sense, talks, and it speaks in many languages. Your learning them will open the road to a new territory.

The Effect of Underclothing

Beneath it all, unseen by the audience, but felt by you, is underclothing. The corset and stays of a more constricted period; the chemise and "teddies" of an unrestricted era, all will contribute to your thoroughly becoming the embodiment of the character. Margaret Dumont attributed part of the interpretation of her "Grand Dame" role in the Marx Brothers movies to the authentic lingerie she wore beneath her gowns.

Underclothes harmonious with the role affect the actor, and investigation of the type of undergarments people wore at the specific time your play is set will prove to be beneficial to you as part of your research and ultimate understanding. Robert De Niro, in the course of re-creating Al Capone in the film *The Untouchables*, learned that Capone wore silk undergarments. De Niro searched out the original source of manufacture and arranged to have the mobster's underwear duplicated. Reinforced by the benefits of authenticity, he then became the veritable gangster.

As you consider each of these examples of accessories, you will recognize how they enable you to form the skin and bones of your character and when variously applied, bring an onslaught of diversified interpretations. Your familiarity and application of the accessories appropriate to the part will add dimension to the role you are undertaking. With them you can expand your horizons in your individual preparation, interweaving their use along with the lines you are absorbing, while becoming accomplished and proficient in their application.

Chapter 4
PROPS

Accessories are joined hand in glove with props. Just as we concentrated on accessories for use in your solitary study, so shall we approach props in the same direction: to avail yourself of easily obtainable props while exploring the character you are assuming.

Alfred Lunt

Once again Alfred Lunt, the perfectionist, must be recalled. While it is not suggested you bear the burden of expense he undertook in order to encompass the most minute details of his part, there is a lesson to be learned in the way you can reach out to establish a total picture which will benefit your performance.

Alfred Lunt was in Chicago to bring to the Second City an Eastern fop in the person of George Tewkesbury Reynolds III who appears in Booth Tarkington's *The Country Cousins*. Since, in Lunt's mind, a proper gentleman required certain staples to announce his quality, before the play opened he ordered a set of visiting cards engraved with George Tewkesbury Reynolds III's imposing name. He had already been to Cartier's where he had purchased a gold cigarette case, with the appropriate initials of G.T.R. III engraved upon the case. A friend of his, alarmed by the degree of such extravagance, could not understand why the actor might not have gone into any store and bought an inexpensive cigarette case since only on one occasion in the play did Reynolds light a cigarette. "Who," his friend inquired of him, "would know the difference?" Lunt's immediate answer was typical: "*I* would."

There are two kinds of props: those giving the actor a reinforced dimension of the role, and the type the actor must learn to use as a direct adjunct to the action.

Dame May Whitty

When Dame May Whitty appeared in Emlyn Williams' play, *Night Must Fall*, she had to use a wheelchair. Not only did it convey to the audience that the woman was crippled, but the wheelchair compelled Dame May to *feel* physically incapacitated. She had to learn how to handle the chair and, in so doing, that prop gave her insight into the limitations imposed upon a person confined to a wheelchair. There are other props that not only help the actor feel handicapped but influence his movements in performance: crutches, a cane, the arm in a splint. All require proficiency in their use and at the same time help an actor to comprehend the character's difficulties and outlook.

There are innumerable small props of ordinary use which are part of the action on stage: a cigarette, a drinking glass, a teapot, a cup and saucer; your imagination can take flight when contemplating the possibilities. Each has to be handled while speaking and applied in the manner appropriate to the character. This is part of your at-home practice, for every one of these small but important props creates an extension and illumination of the character.

The Handkerchief as a Prop

The handkerchief in *Othello* which serves as an accessory to the costume is also a major prop in the play, for if it weren't for the handkerchief Desdemona might have made it to old age. In the scene when Desdemona offers Othello her handkerchief in an attempt to comfort him, he pushes it aside in refusal, and it falls from her hand. As they go off stage, it lies on the floor and the maid Emilia picks it up. At the dress rehearsal of the play in which Uta Hagen portrayed Desdemona, she accidentally dropped the handkerchief too close to her feet, and as she was walking toward the wings, it caught in the train of her dress and trailed away with her. There stood Emilia, with no handkerchief to pick up. Margaret Webster had the role of Emilia, and fortunately she was relieved of the panic that would have ensued had her Emilia been faced with this situation during an actual performance. Without the significant handkerchief, the play would fall apart. But that dress rehearsal taught Margaret Webster the dependance upon even the simplest prop. In all the future performances she had the comfort of a substitute handkerchief tucked up her sleeve, ever ready to "duck behind a chair and pick up what wasn't there."

Just as Desdemona's handkerchief plays the key and dual role of accessory and prop, so does the fan in Oscar Wilde's *Lady Windermere's Fan*; both serve to arouse a husband's suspicions of an unfaithful spouse. Whether the prop or accessory may be major or trivial in the action, their effective use should not be thrown away any more than an actor would throw away a line.

The Umbrella as a Prop

The very manner in which a prop is put to work can serve to interpret a role. Olivier at one time was not comfortable in a particular characterization. During a performance, just before he went on stage, he impulsively picked up a green umbrella that came within his view. As he appeared with it before the audience, swinging it over his shoulder and playing around with the umbrella, he had the sense of his finally having discovered an essential aspect of his part. Later, whenever he sensed that moment in a performance when everything seemed to go as it should, he referred to his having found his green umbrella.

Whether it is a coincidence or, as theatrical anecdotes are related through the years, there is a confusion as to whom one should attribute the event, Alfred Lunt appears to have preceded Olivier with a similar experience. In the course of Lunt's rehearsal as Henry Higgins in Shaw's *Pygmalion*, his interpretation of Higgins' character led to the belief he would be the sort of man who would carry a green umbrella — and no other color would do, but green. Once it was in his possession, Lunt knew that, by George, he had it; he captured the essence of Higgins. From that time on, he used the phrase "green umbrella" as his personal message to Lynn Fontanne that he was attempting to unearth the appropriate prop, accessory or particular detail that would be the keynote of the character.

To whomever belongs the credit of the story, it is nevertheless a verification that both Lunt and Olivier recognized how external components serve as a catalyst.

Props are everywhere, all around you, waiting to be dealt with. And the large ones have to be managed as effectively as the small. The furniture on the set is going to control your action and movement. There is a table to move toward, a couch to sink in, a chair to perch on. How do you sit in a chair? Not everyone sits in one the same way: there are slouchers, straight-as-an-arrow sitters and knee-crossers; the legs-apart sort and the ankles-together type, all a reflection of the person, his manner of dress, and the era in which he lives. Props have their function in determining your character's movements, and you want to set your lines to your dealing with these props.

Real and Artificial Props

There are times when the props aren't exactly what they appear to be. A glass of wine could be raspberry juice; the delicious food you are consuming only an illusion; the photograph you are handed to admire might have nothing to do with the play. But you have to react to these props as if they were the genuine articles. If you take advantage of rehearsing yourself with what is the real thing, when you speak your lines in performance, your imagination and recollection will reinforce you with a sense of the reality. You will give the appearance of extracting taste from nonexistent food, and be able to express genuine admiration for the photograph that isn't there.

Pantomime is built on the remembrance of the factual. The use of real props combined with action heightens all of the senses and ultimately translates them into an indelible memory of sensations.

In Ronald Harwood's play *The Dresser*, Paul Rogers, while portraying an actor putting on his make-up, sat before a mirror which was no mirror, but merely a frame. Without that actual mirror, he applied his make-up, and for him and the audience it was no illusory prop. His familiarity with the application of the make-up before his reflection was sufficient to establish believability without the actual prop. The effect was so powerful that it enabled the audience to use its imagination together with the actor's and see illusion as reality.

Such is the stuff out of which artists are made.

Chapter 5
FABRIC, COLOR
AND LIGHTING

Without emotion and mood there is no theatre. Fabric in all of its textures, color in all of its hues, and lighting in all of its effects, establish and enhance emotion and mood for the actor as well as the audience.

Functions of Texture in Fabrics

Your own response to the touch and feel of the fabric sends a message to your sense of awareness. Run your hand over a length of satin and the word "luxurious," or perhaps the word "sensual," comes into your mind. Touch a soft woolen cloth and feel coziness, warmth and richness; on the contrary, a bristly wool alerts your senses to discomfort and roughness. The contact of burlap provokes the thought of deprivation and poverty. Wear a silk shirt and you experience a quiet refinement; change to a cotton shirt and that sensation disappears. The gentle brush of velvet against the skin and you are imbued with the regal quality of royalty; envelop yourself in furs and luxuriate in its opulence, epitomizing elegance and wealth.

Not only does fabric influence your perceptions, it affects your movements. Notice how differently you wish to walk when you have jersey clinging against your body. Feeling soft and slinky, the fabric almost impels you to move in such a manner. A heavily brocaded garment will slow down your walk, while the flow of chiffon — which can simulate or suggest wind or water — will give you the sensation of floating.

If you are wearing a costume made of a rough cloth, and you are having a scene with an actor who is wearing one of lace, each of you will have different responses towards one another. Not only the type of fabric you wear, but what others are wearing, will affect your reaction, and hence your performance.

Even if your costumes were identical both in style and color but the fabrics were unlike, you would have individual responses and employ your costumes in a different manner. In Jean Anouilh's *The Lark* the Dominican monks are all dressed in the same black and white habits, and their nature is necessarily stern. But one among them, Brother Ladvenu, is gentle and pitying. The only way in which he can be distinguished, as they all kneel, sit or stand together, is for his habit to be of a fabric less rigid than those of the others. Therefore, while the other monks are dressed in habits of stiff fabrics reflecting their attitude, Brother Ladvenu wears one of soft, pliant black cashmere. The actor portraying Brother Ladvenu, taking advantage of the expressiveness of this gentle fabric, is able to establish the contrast between his tender nature and those of the austere monks. And although from outward appearance, all seem alike, the fabric and its effect upon the actor verifies the difference. Fabric acts.

Functions of Color in Fabrics

Color and fabric are interwoven, and the impact of color upon the actor as well as the audience is manifold, for it is part of the fabric of our lives. As infants, our first awareness is light, then color. The feeling for color and its influence upon our emotions continues throughout our lives. We hope for or admire a "colorful" life, and all of the major events we experience are marked by color.

Infancy brings its first use. White is the symbol of purity and innocence, and the pastels of pinks, blues and yellows signify naïvete and youth. First, the traditional white christening dress, then the pink prom dress, followed by the white bridal gown. Older years bring darker, rich colors of deep reds, purples and black which represent sophistication, knowledge and power. Black is the standard for funerals, connoting death. From our white innocent beginning to the finality of black, all these stages are stamped with color and its effect upon our emotions follows us all through our days.

Individual colors impart distinct expressions. Yellow, the symbol of sunlight, suggests joy. Red alludes to brilliance as well, but one of excitement, and the devil himself is summoned up in our imagination by the show of red. Purple almost automatically suggests royalty.

White shines, yellow glows, and black dies. Not only does color communicate with our eyes, but it has its own peculiar sound. Red screams, grey whispers, black cries. Color is music: it plays, it sings. Color acts.

The playwright's ideas must be put in visual form, and color is the illustration of the emotions he is conveying in words, reacting upon both the actor and the audience. It sets the mood, illuminates the characters.

Alla Nazimova

The Russian actress, Alla Nazimova, attributed particular colors to the type of individual. She believed that once an actress knew the character well enough to be aware of what she is thinking and her inner responses, she would know that she would never choose to wear red nor tie a pink bow in her hair, but rather would be a blonde who would elect to wear gray. Wearing gray and being blonde, she would naturally move in a particular way and speak with a certain inflection. However, from a practical viewpoint, she knew that if her own idea of the character's color preferences did not come to fruition in the production and she was compelled to portray her as a brunette, she would imagine herself to be blonde, and pretend she was clad in grey while wearing a golden-haired wig.

Laurette Taylor

But Laurette Taylor, on opening night of *The Glass Menagerie*, could not be so swayed as to pretend color, so important did she feel the proper shade was necessary to her interpretation. She had not been satisfied with the color of the dressing gown she was to wear in a later scene of the first act. When a member of the production staff opened her dressing room door to peer in to give her last call for the curtain and to wish her well, he saw her bending over a dark, soggy mass of material in the wash basin. On her way to the stage, she pushed this dripping bundle into his hands with a firm order to dry it. She had decided that she could not go on with what she felt was the wrong color for the dressing gown and dyed it. It was left to the now-distraught staff member to find whatever means he could to dry it in time for Laurette Taylor's Amanda to put on her dressing gown of a more suitable hue.

41

Color and Mood

There are times when an actor may be given a costume in a shade originally felt to be correct, then have the same costume changed to another color because the director, along with the costume and lighting designers, realizes the second choice works better for the mood of the scene and results in achieving a better reaction from the actor. The color not only has to be appropriate for the mood of the scene, it also has to be appropriate for the mood of the actor.

In a production of *Richard III*, Laurence Olivier was in a costume of brown and black before he met with Lady Anne. For the salubrious occasion of being with her, he exchanged those somber colors for a costume in deep red trimmed with white lace. But when they parted and he next said his prayers with the bishops, he returned to his brown and black costume, its subdued nature more in keeping with prayer. The correctness of color to the occasion reflected the mood of the scene as well as the actor's emotion.

Just as types of fabric in the same color convey differences in the temperament and character portrayed, so two actors in the same costume but in different colors will exact a change of reaction. The girl in a red velvet gown will evoke a dissimilar emotion than a girl in the same style of costume but in pale pink or aqua.

The identical shade of red in a variety of fabric textures, as in the case of black-robed monks, will exhibit varying attributes. While red velvet suggests elegance, red satin may indicate cheap lewdness and red chiffon graceful sensuality. The effects of the combination of color and fabric upon the actor as well as the audience are manifold, for color paints a picture of the person's character.

Each period in history has its popular colors which animate the time, place and people. When Ruth Gordon appeared in William Wycherley's *The Country Wife* in London at the Old Vic, she and costume designer Oliver Messel discussed her character, Marjory Pinchwife. He suggested that since she was mousy, she'd wear drab clothes. But Ruth Gordon saw it differently. "Country people," she said, "are gaudy. They like colors that show." She

Laurence Olivier in Richard III

believed Mrs. Simpson, because she was from the city, would choose beige, but that country folk preferred candy pink, buttercup yellow, and poppy red.

43

Color, Fabric and Lighting

As interwoven as color and fabric is the marriage of lighting and color, and lighting adds its brand of magic to the reaction and mood of the actor as well as the audience. Envision the play of candlelight on satin or velvet in an eighteenth-century scene of an otherwise dark room in *Les Liaisons Dangereuses*, or the brilliance of chandeliers in the early twentieth-century ballroom scene of Alan Jay Lerner and Frederick Loewe's musical *My Fair Lady*. Two varying emotions stir your heart. Stage lighting has the ability to change the tones of a costume and the mood of an actor. Along with fabric and color, light acts too.

When treated with fluorescent paints, there are certain fabrics that glow in the dark as a filtered ultraviolet light, known as black light, is focused on them. With the stage in total darkness, all that can be seen are these colors which, painted on cloth, create a variety of effects, from dancing skeletons to white-gloved hands moving in the air. Costumes so treated appear to be moving without people in them. This lighting effect was used to great advantage in musical extravaganzas of the past, and continues to be employed.

Props as well as costumes can be fluorescently lighted, and before World War II the English comedian, Lupino Lane, built an act based on this principle. In a London production of *The Golden Toy*, he appeared on a darkened stage. With a lone spotlight focusing upon him, he climbed upon a fluorescent-painted rope. When he reached the arch of the theatre and out of the spotlight, all that remained in sight was the rope in midair, and he appeared to have evaporated.

The impact of this type of lighting upon the audience is always one of great surprise and delight, and the performer, wearing these treated costumes, is the keeper of the secret and the surprise. This produces a very particular result for the actor and his movements, and usually translates into a merry mood for all.

An actor utilizing all the infinite combinations for fabric, color and light, is able to originate and achieve dramatic effects otherwise beyond his reach. He acts with fabric; he acts with color; he acts with light.

Chapter 6
SUITABILITY AND COMFORT

The costume should be an enrichment to the character as a dress should be to a woman: to enhance but not to distract. An actor thus endowed has an ally in his theatrical clothing.

The Problems of Improper Costuming

Can a costume be so overpowering in design that it diminishes the performance? Yes. Sometimes the designer is carried away and the result is an overpowering costume: perhaps too brilliant in color, too intricate in design, or incorrect in fabric texture to suit the emotion of the play. This can detract from an actor's performance. When both the actor and the audience are too aware of the costume, the acting becomes secondary, or as unsuitable as the wardrobe.

Laurette Taylor's mother was a fine dressmaker, and frequently supplied the costumes for her daughter. This was a double blessing, since actors at that time were financially responsible for them. When the Shuberts were producing *The Ringmaster* and Laurette Taylor was appearing in the lead as Eleanor Hillary, they would not permit her mother to make the costumes, but insisted upon a particular currently popular designer to do so — all at Laurette's cost, in more ways than one.

For the first act she wore a dress overcome with white polka dots ranging in scale from pin point to dollar size. It was topped by a huge rose-colored velvet bow with two gigantic rhinestones, reminding Laurette Taylor of headlights on a car, and that thought clung to her throughout that opening act.

The second act's costume presented her with a problem. The dress had a train in which the designer placed weights so that the train would spread out behind her. Since the stage had no carpeting, as she walked the train's weights would set up a clatter as they hit the bare boards. She decided to move as little as possible to avoid the distraction.

A new hazard was created by the third act costume, which was a salmon-pink dress covered from top to toe with tiny bugle-shaped spangles. It was the climax of the play, wherein Eleanor denounced her father while shaking a newspaper in front of his face. As she did so, the little bugle spangles gave off tinkling sounds. Finally, when she threw the newspaper on a nearby table in an irate gesture, the spangles poured forth a torrent of tinkles. At that point she dared not move and stood rigid, depending solely upon her voice to register all the emotions of the scene. Despite all of her efforts, Laurette Taylor felt certain that she appeared to be a bad actress, due to her problem-filled costumes.

The critics agreed with the actress's assessment of her performance, and the critic Charles Darnton reported that "Miss Laurette Taylor was so completely at sea in the role of Eleanor Hillary and so loaded with clothes of strange design that you felt like throwing her an anchor."

With this lesson learned by Laurette Taylor, she took scrupulous care not to fall victim again, and became innovative in her costuming when she believed it necessary for the sense of the play. When she played the role of Portia in *The Merchant of Venice*, she was convinced that Bassanio's inability to recognize Portia during the trial scene made no sense unless she were sufficiently disguised. So, contrary to Portia's customary appearance, the actress darkened her complexion with make-up, set a black wig on her head instead of the usual golden hair of Portia, and wore the doublet and hose of an Italian lawyer. As she studied herself in the mirror, she had confidence that she was a convincing and appropriately attired Portia.

Costumes Must be Appropriate to Role

Suitability of costuming to the text is essential, not only to the play, but for the actor's proper interpretation. For good or evil, the costume's influence upon the actor is enormous. There have been many disasters impressed upon helpless performers by unintelligent costuming and, no matter how hard they try, the acting is made either ridiculous or subservient to the costume. In a Metropolitan Opera production of Giacomo Puccini's *Turandot* some of its finest singers were presented in so unsuitably elaborate costuming that the audience and the artists were completely overwhelmed by them, and the singing almost went unnoticed. In one scene the soprano appeared with a dazzling, pompom-trimmed candelabra on her head and a backpack of scrolls resting on her shoulders. As a costume more appropriate for musical comedy than operatic drama, it became the center of the performance, overshadowing the soprano's great aria and provoking laughter from the audience.

From the most esteemed productions to a traveling troupe, a badly designed or poorly conceived costume can depreciate a performer's work to the same degree as an actor who does not properly use his costume can diminish the quality of his performance. Margaret Webster was working with a bus and truck production of *Hamlet*, and she believed it was unsatisfactory because the fabrics of the costumes were too lightweight for such an austere drama.

There are many times when an actor finds himself having to take on responsibility for his costume when it is a matter of his conviction that his acting depends upon its suitability. When Richard Burton appeared in the play *Equus* by Peter Shaffer, he succeeded Anthony Perkins and wore the exact copy of the suit worn by his predecessor. After several performances, Burton discovered that under the lights the color was too pale for him and the suit's fabric too stiff. He viewed the character of Dysart as a doctor so dedicated and hardworking, that he would give little thought to his appearance. Therefore, he chose to wear one of his own rumpled, very much used suits.

Costumes and Comfort

An actor must be comfortable in his wardrobe to be comfortable in his role. Shoes must be both correct in appearance and correct in fit; the waistline easy. The actor, as well as the dancer, must have comfort together with freedom for necessary physical action. Of course, this does not hold true in every instance. There are costumes that call for physical restraint and particular posture, and in these circumstances they serve as an aid to the actor and his actions. Appropriateness and suitability is the primary rule.

Aside from physical comfort, there is the ease that comes from knowing the costume is perfect in every detail and therefore an assistance to the performance. When Alfred Lunt and Lynn

Fontanne appeared in *The Visit*, he portrayed the degraded has-been. And although the shabby old suit he wore sufficiently conveyed his state, Alfred Lunt, despite the fact that he never was called upon to remove his shoes during the course of the play, wore socks darned at the toe and heel. To him, this was a form of comfort and suitability knowing that he was wearing something additionally indicative of the character.

In a similar situation, when Lee Strasberg appeared in the film *The Godfather II*, he was directed to wear a brown suit, and he wore matching brown socks. The director then changed his mind and decided that Strasberg should wear a black suit instead. Strasberg requested a pair of black socks to match the color of the suit but he was told that it was not important since the socks would not be visible. But before they filmed the scene, he insisted on changing to black socks for the simple and important reason that they made him feel correctly dressed.

With comfort and suitability as part of his costume, the actor has yet another spur to his performance.

Chapter 7
POSTURE

Costumes, accessories and props all lead to the emergence of the total appearance, and to complete the picture you must know how to deal with all these elements in the style which they dictate.

You might be adorned in the most beautiful of gowns with a magnificent train, but if you are not holding your body in an erect, stately fashion and, when you turn, your feet get caught up and twisted in the train, you are not doing credit to yourself or your costume.

John Gielgud's admiration for actress Gwen Frangcon Davies was partially based upon her assistance to him whenever they performed together. Furthermore, he was greatly impressed by the fact that she left nothing to chance. When she appeared with him in the role of Anne in *Richard of Bordeaux*, she carefully studied her costumes so that she could be fortified with the knowledge as to where they could help or possibly hinder her during a performance. In rehearsal she always wore a train, and executed every sweep of her dress and movement of her body skillfully and gracefully.

The Actor's Mastery of the Costume

But the actress who was queen to Maurice Evans in a production of *Richard II* had not the foresight to be so well prepared. The actress was timid and inexperienced in the use of the trains of her gown; all she could accomplish was getting her feet wrapped in them. Rehearsal had to come to a halt so the director, Margaret Webster, could give her an emergency lesson on how to control the trains.

In the same play, other actors had different problems, all relating to their lack of preparation in the mastery of their costumes. The men wore cloaks and hadn't the slightest notion of what to do with them other than just let the cloaks hang drearily from their necks. Everything was at a standstill because the actors

49

did not learn beforehand to understand and handle the essential costumes. There could be no play until they could move themselves correctly and appropriately in their cloaks and trains.

As an actress Margaret Webster appreciated the need for learning the proper way in which clothing should be worn. During her early years in the theatre, she had the small part of Miss Fanny in James Barrie's *Quality Street* which was being presented at London's Haymarket, and she worked hard to portray the part with authenticity. She took the necessary path to the museums to examine prints and drawings to find out how the clothes were worn, how the shawl was draped, right down to the correct tilt of a bonnet.

Margaret Webster's mother was actress Dame May Whitty, and daughter Margaret continued the family's acting tradition. Her theatre-steeped life shaped well-formed opinions and capabil-

50

ities. Using her acting experience as the spur, ultimately Margaret Webster turned toward a different phase of the theatre, and became a director. In discussing another acting family, brother and sister Fred and Ellen Terry, she evaluated Fred Terry's skill in handling his costume. In her estimation, no one could wear a square cut coat and lace ruffles, white wig and rapier with his grace, dash, and virile magnificence. What impressed her in particular was his facility to move in the clothing he wore in performance as if they were actually the clothes he put on when he arose from his bed each morning. He wore them, not as if they comprised a costume, but his own usual apparel.

Costume Construction Affects Actor's Movements

Not only does the costume demand that you use it properly, there are certain garments and underpinnings that compel their proper use. Women's period clothing requires corsets and corset covers, padding for busts, back-ends and hips. The corsets are boned to keep the bodice smooth, the padding to give the illusion of a small waist. If it is a dress of the mid-nineteenth century, a foundation consisting of three or more hoops graduating in size from the hipline to the hemline is then placed over the waist and hips — a contraption to be reckoned with. Covering all that is a petticoat, and possibly over the petticoat an underskirt pleated or ruffled along the bottom. Finally the smooth, snug-fitting bodice of the dress along with the overskirt covers all of these underwrappings. If you attempt to move and sit in these layers as you do in your everyday clothing, you have a disaster ahead.

A late twentieth-century woman, now attired in these tiers of restricting fashion, can no longer move in her accustomed free and easy strides. She is the upright, slender-waisted, gracefully gliding woman of another age. Her costume has changed her appearance and she becomes a creature of the past, together with a new feeling which makes unexpected demands of her. She must now learn anew how to sit, stand and walk and, in addition, achieve the ability to gesture with her hands, wrists and elbows, all necessitated by the rigidity of the upper part of her body and the impediments of her skirts.

Period Costumes Require Practice

Yet, although this alien clothing and its accoutrements may

at the onset be clumsy to handle in its strange requirements, with practiced use it renders unto the wearer a fragile, feminine charm that is synonymous with the period. But it does take preparation. It is perfectly natural for an actress, accustomed to wearing pants in everyday life as well as in rehearsal, to stumble over the front of her hoop skirt the first time she wears it. Therefore it might serve her better, while learning her lines and in rehearsal, to forego the pants and instead wear a long dirndl skirt, and begin to capture the proper movements and step by step graduate into the intricacies of hoop, petticoats and skirts. The role will also require sitting in a hoop skirt which must collapse like a Japanese lantern as she settles herself upon a chair. Therefore, the actress must learn to sit in a way utterly different than her own.

The actor who is going to sit in an armchair wearing an eighteenth-century skirted coat and dress sword while carrying a tricorn hat under his arm has much to accomplish as well. On his way into settling himself into the chair, he doesn't want to stab himself on his own sword while trying to figure out what to do with his hat. Neither does he want to forget about his coattails and crumple them as he sits down. And, with all this going on, he certainly doesn't want to knock over the chair.

Costumes Affect Posture

The actor must learn to combine the character, period and costume in every stance, whether sitting, standing or walking. It is at this point an actor should with all speed research the period of the play and intently study in the museums paintings of the posturing of the day. It will acquaint the actor in the management of the garments as well as an aid to achieving the correct bearing.

From one era to another the clothing of each period affected the posture. Note the bearing of a gentleman of the Roman Empire in his toga and the contrasting carriage of a seventeenth-century cavalier wearing a flowing cape and a large ostrich-plumed hat. (See illustrations on page 50.) Study a painting of a man in a tricorn hat with plumes of the Louis XVI period, his light turquoise coat with jabot, lace wrist cuffs, handkerchief, ruffles, white wig and jeweled rings. Then observe a painting of Daniel Boone in his leather jacket and raccoon tail hat and compare the difference in their stance. Obviously their clothing has molded their postures. An actor dressed as Monsieur Beaucaire will neither feel nor move as he would in frontiersman's clothing.

The dignified steeple headdress and veil of the fifteenth century, its shape fashioned upon and mirroring the solemnity of the spired churches and stained glass of the Middle Ages, requires an extraordinarily different posture than what would be required of a person wearing a cloche hat along with a short skirt of the Twenties. To exchange postures is unthinkable, unless comedy is your aim.

Costumes Are an Aid, Not an Encumbrance

Through all of this, despite the new demands it makes upon you, the costume is not to be regarded as an encumbrance to be overcome, but a major step toward developing the person you are becoming. Who has not been enchanted by Vivien Leigh's portrayal of Scarlet in *Gone With the Wind*? She moved with such

grace and ease we readily believed she actually lived during the Civil War period, so did her movement in costume become second nature to her.

When Joshua Logan was directing the Richard Rodgers and Oscar Hammerstein musical, *The King and I*, and the performers found the necessary actions and movements completely foreign to them and impossible to acquire, he reassured them that when they were in costume, it would all come to them naturally. But first they had to learn to be natural in the costumes.

Your goal is to learn to live in your costume as if it were your usual form of dress. When you have reached the point where you are utterly at home in your acquired clothing and you have mastered the correct way to sit, stand and walk, there is still another attainment to be negotiated. And that is to use it all to proper dramatic effect.

A Canadian production of Gilbert and Sullivan's *The Mikado* underscored the manner in which a familiar theatre piece can become brand new when costumes are handled by performers in a way to create effects that introduce another element. The singer-actors gave a sense of constant movement and drama by the swirling, dipping, sweeping motions of their robes, sleeves and trains while adroitly maneuvering fans. All of this motion through costume unfolded a tale of romance, joy, tragedy, comedy and triumph, and achieved convincing, exciting theatre.

Imaginatively handled by actors, trains, capes, shawls and drapery yield performances of tremendous impact. When the actor establishes intimacy with his costume and knows all of its possibilities, he can both feel and convey deep emotion.

Chapter 8
MASKS, MAKE-UP AND DISGUISES

One doesn't have to be in the theatre to use and appreciate make-up. One of our first morning acts is to examine ourselves in the mirror and then set about putting on the face which is familiar to others.

"A little powder, a little paint, makes a girl what she ain't." Add to that the help of a comb, and a woman is ready to present herself as she wishes to be recognized. A man's razor removes a night's growth of stubble. If he possesses a moustache or beard which he acquired for an altered aspect, he gives it a shaping up for the day. With the further assistance of his hairbrush, he has prepared his appearance before the world.

These are light disguises which we all use for displaying the public side of ourselves. However, in the world of theatre, when the actor becomes another individual, the disguise must be complete. Make-up is an element of the costume that accomplishes the total alteration.

To establish a sense of either reality or fantasy in the theatre it is necessary to apply a form of camouflage. The first theatrical production may have taken place centuries ago in the temples of East India where chosen maidens played the roles of goddesses and were so masqueraded. Carefully groomed film stars of the past were dubbed "movie goddesses"; perhaps it was an off-shoot reference to the contrived lure of those East Indian maiden goddesses.

Masks Obliterate Personal Identity

The shaman should also be credited for his part in the dawn of theatre. Medicine men used masks and make-up to hide their true identities to become the sought-after image. As theatre advanced, the mask served as the cover of the real person and an indication of the personality being presented. Each individual's mask informed the audience whether the character was good or

57

evil, of his desires, if he was happy or filled with sorrow, and beneath that representational mask the actor governed himself according to the one he held to his face. His simple costume, consisting of only that mask, influenced his acting. With it the actor masked his own feelings and assumed those of someone else, completely believable to himself and the audience.

Disguise obliterates personal identity and helps the actor assume another. Acting in itself is a concealment of the person who is the actor, hiding his own likeness. He must, in a sense, regard himself as a slate rubbed clean, upon which another image appears through the use of disguise or make-up. Camouflage and make-up, synonymous with costume, complete the act of disappearance of one person and then emergence into another.

Richard Kiley

Richard Kiley found it difficult to play Joe Rose in *A Month of Sundays* and David Jordan in Richard Rodgers' *No Strings* because the roles called for contemporary, everyday clothing. He felt more comfortable in costume and make-up since they allowed him to hide behind them, enabling him to forget his own personality and dedicate it instead to the character. He cherished the turbans and flashy satins he wore as the Caliph in *Kismet*; the Don Quixote cape in *Man of La Mancha* became his permanent, natural garment.

Through years of acting, Kiley has discovered that the more costumes and make-up he has, the more his comfort increases to the benefit of his performance. During a discussion he had with Laurence Olivier, they concurred in the freedom each experienced when in disguise, and Olivier's device of concealing himself behind a nose, eyebrows, or some kind of make-up is well known.

Disguises Help Actors Overcome Inhibitions

Despite the fact that well-known performers appear confident on stage, there are many who suffer from shyness. Costume and make-up not only help in the development of the role, but they become the refuge of the shy and form a protective shell which helps to overcome inhibitions. Scenic and costume designer Oliver Messel had created masks which intrigued Emlyn Williams. When he placed one after the other over his face he lost his self-consciousness, and discovered while hidden beneath those masks he was able to produce a variety of men's and women's voices. Later, when he performed in a one-man show as Charles Dickens, the Dickens beard became a cover for this timidity.

John Gielgud

In creating and building his make-up, the actor continues to develop and reveal the character, becoming totally immersed until he is at one with that other being. When John Gielgud was a young man he was given a role depicting someone his own age. He was aware of showing his own personality, and found it difficult to keep inside the character. As with many young actors, he was self-conscious. Subsequently, when he appeared at the Oxford Playhouse as Trofimov in Anton Chekhov's *The Cherry Orchard*, he discovered that the make-up he developed erased his inhibitions, making him easy and confident with his newly acquired personality. He selected a black wig that was thin on the top and front, put on a small beard and wore steel-rimmed glasses. As he studied his changed reflection in the mirror, he knew exactly how Trofimov would move, speak and behave. Throughout his performance he kept that image firmly in mind, and lost himself completely in his appearance and in the action of the play.

An actor who avoids disguise is himself playing a role, relying upon his own physical aspects or personal magnetism. A critic had noted that Jessica Tandy and Hume Cronyn in Brian Clark's *The Petition* projected their own winning ways, but when Mr. Cronyn utilizes disguises in his masterly fashion, it is apparent that he is one of the best character actors in the theatre.

Disguises Provide Multiple Choices

It is inherent in the actor to wish to become someone else, and disguises give him multiple choices in the opportunity to cover himself, but first he must acquire the ability to create and use them. Ralph Richardson always designed his make-up before applying it and began by making studied detailed drawings, including all the shadows and highlights. It is necessary to be meticulous in camouflage as in all aspects of performance. As an actor, you already know that regardless of your desire to be someone else, it is not an easy thing to do, but the costume and make-up are there, waiting for you to put them to useful advantage.

As a youth, John Gielgud longed to possess a photograph of Edith Evans as she truly was, without costume or make-up. He was not sure what she looked like since she always resembled the part she was playing. She learned to form with cosmetics any character she chose, using her own face as a canvas. So successful were her transformations, her own natural appearance was a matter of conjecture to the young Gielgud.

Lon Chaney

There are those actors whose varied appearances so completely submerged their own personalities that theatrical history has permanently identified them with these altered appearances, and their performances have become classics. In silent films, Lon Chaney, an actor known for his superb artistry in make-up, undertook the creation of many unforgettable characters including *The Hunchback of Notre Dame* and *The Phantom of the Opera*. He earned the designation of "the man with a thousand faces."

José Ferrer

José Ferrer is joined permanently in memory with Toulouse Lautrec and Cyrano de Bergerac. Hal Holbrook and Mark Twain will forever be entwined. In portraying famous individuals, believable appearance is an essential; imagination and extraordinary acting nevertheless require disguise. This is not an indication that an actor depending upon disguise and make-up alone automatically becomes the character. Never take them for granted in their ability to help you in your delineation. It means that along with the costume, the actor learns to use them fully and appropriately while developing his role. Put him in the most suitable costume and disguise, and if he hasn't acquired the art of handling them properly, he hasn't succeeded in his total immersion.

Paul Muni

Paul Muni's genius sprouted when he was a child actor and, as it grew, he experimented with make-up and perfected it for each of the varied roles he undertook throughout his career in the theatre and film. During his boyhood days in the Yiddish theatre, Muni was assigned the roles of old men, and behind his beard and his costume, he was completely convincing. But he was after all, a youngster with the playfulness that goes along with

Lon Chaney in The Phantom of the Opera.

childhood, and among his pleasures was roller-skating. Since several performances were given during the course of the day, it wasn't practical to remove costume and make-up. So, in between shows, without bothering to even remove his beard, young Muni would be seen roller-skating in the alley behind the theatre in his old-man costume. The ancient figure that brought tears to the eyes now elicited laughter at what became an incongruous

José Ferrer as Toulouse Lautrec in Moulin Rouge.

sight. He was no longer realistically using his costume, and no beard or rumpled old-man clothing could make him anything but what he was: a child having fun on his roller skates.

Make-up and Lighting

In an era when the stagelights illuminating the scene con-

José Ferrer as Cyrano de Bergerac.

sisted of candlelight, the simple purpose of make-up was to enable the actor's face to be clearly seen. With the advent of other forms of stage lighting, including oil and gas, which eventually put the actor "in the limelight," the problem of the fading out of the features of the performer's face persisted. In order to overcome this handicap produced by the lighting, the actors were obliged to apply make-up with a heavy hand and employed exaggerated expressions so that they could be carried beyond the overpowering footlights to the audience. Since lighting is subtle today, such heavy make-up is no longer required unless it is necessary for particular effect.

Make-up in its present form is a refined art, and is a basic essential, not only because lighting continues to demand its use, but because make-up has the ability to immediately define the age, health, sex, race, traits, manner and profession of the character. Make-up combined with the costume is indispensable in order to prepare the actor psychologically, so that he is completely and perfectly submerged in becoming and being another person. Acting of even the highest degree cannot overcome the lack of accentuation of the face, for it reflects, along with the clothing, all of the elements of the person portrayed.

Make-up Artistry

The theatre actor, unlike the film actor, is responsible for his own make-up and, in acquiring this responsibility, is aided through his use of make-up in developing his role. If the budget allows, there are times when a professional make-up artist is required not only to create the original make-up, but also any special effects necessary to fulfill the director's conception. Andrew Lloyd Webber's musical, *Cats*, is a stylized production completely dependent upon costume and make-up to transform the actors into members of the feline world, and requires the handiwork of the make-up professional.

In *The Apple Tree* by Jerry Bock and Sheldon Harnick, because Barbara Harris played distinctly different characters with little time between acts to change the make-up, the make-up designer devised an ingenious method of layered make-up. Without the craftsmanship of professional backup, the actress's various interpretations would have been diminished.

Big River gives the impression of having a tremendous cast, when in actuality there are only twenty-one people. Since some actors assumed as many as five or six different parts requiring many costume changes, there had to be just as many make-up changes to complete the illusion of a variety of types. All had to be accomplished quickly and easily because of the many instances when an actor had to be off and promptly on-stage again as another personality, which made a change of make-up almost impossible. The solution was found in the person of a dentist who specialized in cosmetic dentistry. He created dental inserts that provided "hillbilly" teeth, "English" teeth, protruding teeth, even a harelip, all shaped with such distinctiveness they were visible to the audience. Once an actor popped an insert in his mouth, and quickly added one of a variety of wigs, beards and hair pieces along with costume changes, he could immediately react to the impact of becoming another character and act accordingly.

Through the course of continuing performances, it is the actor who must apply his make-up, and the actor is bereft of one of his important tools if he has not become skilled in the art of make-up.

Alfred Lunt

After the Lunts returned to New York from their journey to Budapest and London to prepare their roles in *The Guardsman*, Alfred Lunt wanted to put his guardsman to the test. After all, if he was to disguise himself as an army officer in an attempt to seduce his nonsuspecting wife, he had to be certain he was believably unrecognizable to the woman who knew him intimately. A former Russian officer, now turned doorman at a hotel in Budapest, served as his role model. With military haircut and an accent accomplished as a result of studying the doorman, Lunt, dressed in a modified guardsman's guise, visited the neighborhood grocer who the Lunts knew through steady patronage. The grocer viewed the Russian-accented officer with the usual disinterest of a New York merchant, never for a moment even capturing a glimmer of resemblance between the uniformed officer and his long-time customer. Alfred Lunt knew that he had successfully passed the test of a complete disguise. Since he fooled the grocer, he was assured that he could believably deceive his wife into accepting him as a Russian officer and not her own husband.

Therefore, make-up serves the actor not only as a physical means of appearing as another person, but it enables him to actually shape and evolve into the character and, together with the clothing he is wearing, bring him completely to life.

Disability Disguises

Disguise and make-up also highlight a character's physical disabilities when they are important to the action. The role of

65

Porgy in George and Ira Gershwin's *Porgy and Bess* requires the actor to appear crippled, and it is an essential delineation of his character. The actor could not possibly create Porgy without the disguise of disabled legs.

Wigs and Hair Styles

Wigs are part of make-up, but that does not preclude an actor, whenever possible, from changing his own hair style. It may be as simple as parting hair in the center to something as drastic as Yul Brynner's decision to shave off his hair to become the King of Siam. When an actor's make-up and hair style are his own responsibility, his dedication leads him to research what is appropriate to the character and the time in which he lives. An actor's work is never done!

Creative Choices

Creativity always reigns, for that is of what artistry consists. An actor can sit before a mirror and determine whether the character would be better personified with a beard or a moustache, and so go on to fashion him. There are those actors who would prefer not to wear a false beard or moustache, and once the decision has been made, rely upon growing their own. Putting on or losing weight makes alterations in features as well as the body and thereupon assists in still another kind of transformation. These decisions, of course, rest with the playwright and director, as well as the actor.

Simon Callow

Simon Callow, who originated the role of Mozart in the London production of *Amadeus*, was called upon to portray the title role in Brecht's *The Resistible Rise of Arturo Ui*. He had no problem in adapting himself to his costume consisting of oversized suit, shirt and shoes, with a hump built into the jacket of the suit. White gloves and a dusty, obvious wig added to the perfection of the costume. But when it came to finding the right face to go with it, he ran into difficulty since white paint, black eyebrows and red lips were not what he wanted. At the point of panic and despair as opening night approached, he searched among the various and sundry gimmicks resting in his make-up box. He found a joke-shop false nose and Hitler moustache combination on an elastic. As he put it over the wig, the elastic stretched across his face, splitting up the face in a peculiar fashion. It was nothing he had envisioned before, but with his experimentation he created the abstract creature he now knew was exactly what he had been unknowingly looking for.

To Convince an Audience the Actor Must Convince Himself

Laurence Olivier's visualization of the character he was to portray had often been focused upon the kind of nose that person would likely have, and constructed one, since noses are indeed often indicative of the individual. Even if he did not actually apply putty to his own nose, with the ability to envision what it should be, he began the development of the person he was establishing.

Make-up does not always have to consist of dramatic changes. Peter Sellers and Alec Guinness have always used their make-up in subtle fashion, combining facial expressiveness along with the make-up, but nevertheless it had to be a mixture of both. Swoozie Kurtz in *The House of Blue Leaves* by John Guare, appearing almost innocent of make-up which in its quiet way was there, wearing a dreary, shabby sweater covering a nondescript nightgown, created a pathetically lost soul. But the change must be there lest the actor portray himself and not the character, and he must know how to use that change to be effective and persuasive.

When Sarah Bernhardt played the role of Cleopatra, she stained her hands with henna. Fellow actress, Mrs. Patrick Campbell, questioned her purpose since out front the audience would not clearly see her hands nor note the difference. "No," said Sarah, "But I shall." All must be in harmony to be correct: the actor, the costume, the make-up.

Your ultimate object is to master your costume's uses and become one with it, assume a face and shape consistent with the character, view yourself in the mirror, and see another person. With that accomplishment, you will be able to do anything that person can do.

PART II:
IMPROVISATION AND INNOVATIVE COSTUMING

Chapter 9
COMEDIANS AND COSTUME IDENTITIES

Inappropriate costume or misuse of a costume becomes comedy. A young woman in boy's clothing serves as a disguise to hide her feminine identity, a device often used in opera. But a young woman dressed as a boy can be an amusing figure, as Molly Picon demonstrated when she was the star of Yiddish comedy theatre. Put a young man in a woman's costume as Shakespeare's theatre did, and he can become a convincing Ophelia. If comedian Milton Berle dressed as Ophelia, he would produce comedy.

La Cage Aux Folles has become a musical comedy standard, and a great part of its success rests with the presentation of men dressed as women. It also reinforces the necessity of correct use of costumes normally associated with the opposite sex in order to create distinct identities and illusion. The "girls" in the dance line-up in the musical are completely acceptable to themselves and the audience as real, live girls rather than the men they actually are, suggesting them by their costumes and deportment. They are so completely identifiable as bona fide chorus girls that, as an added spoof, in the chorus line is indeed a real, live girl. Part of the fun of the show is to try to pick her out, but it's not easy to do. On the other hand, the lead of *La Cage Aux Folles* is an outrageously extravagant characterization, and his costuming leaves no doubt that he is a man dressed as a woman so as to create a comedic figure.

Tootsie is a film that also is based upon transsexual dress, although its premise is different. Dustin Hoffman as Tootsie is laughable only to the audience who knows he is a man disguised as a woman; but to the people whose lives Tootsie touches, there is no disguise. Tootsie is accepted as a woman. In theatrical cross-dressing the line is thin between obvious comedy and completely believable disguise.

Marilyn Monroe's *Some Like It Hot* has become a movie classic.

71

Tony Curtis in female disguise as her "girlfriend," and Jack Lemmon in his feminine garb receiving loving devotion from Joe E. Brown, dispensed comedy through their hilarious use of costume camouflage.

Tony Curtis and Jack Lemmon in Some Like It Hot.

In *Victor/Victoria*, Julie Andrews deftly handled an even more complex role of a woman impersonating a man, flip-flopping into an accepted male figure disguised as a female. How could it have been done without costume as her inspiration and concealment?

Making the most of the costume dictates the result of the performance, so it is of utmost importance to know how to handle garments worn by the opposite sex, either authentically or comically, inasmuch as the clothing is a vital key to character identity. James M. Barrie's eternal Peter Pan is always played by a woman in boys clothing; both audience and performers accept without doubt that the actress is a magical young lad.

The Marx Brothers

It was out of preposterous use of costume that special identities emerged. The Marx Brothers became examples of the ability of costume, make-up and props to construct a comic character. Groucho had his black moustache, a cigar, and mobile bushy eyebrows. Harpo and his harp would have produced no comedy without his red wig, battered top hat and oversized raincoat. Chico and his piano became distinctive with his peaked hat. Only Zeppo faded out of the comedy; he wore no gimmick-turned-comedic.

Outlandish dress has often become hallmarks of comedians: loud, oversized plaids, padded out "fat" costumes, and the varieties of clown outfits. Well-known costume trademarks of great comedians had a definitive effect upon their performances. Over many years they relied on those costumes which became a complete part of them, another skin.

Charlie Chaplin

Charlie Chaplin became an enduring figure when he created Charlie the Tramp and he is another illustration of how an actor is able to build a character through the use of costume. He related that he had no preconceived ideas, and it was only when he dressed in his derby, baggy pants, tight jacket and moustache that he began to recognize what he was accomplishing. By the time he walked onto the movie set the tramp was fully born. When he appeared before producer Mack Sennett he assumed the character and strutted about, swinging his cane. At that moment, gags and comedy ideas began racing through his mind. The total inspiration was in the costume.

A tramp is out of character if he wears a tuxedo, since it is an attempt of his desire to show himself to be a member of the upper classes, and both Charlie Chaplin and Judy Garland established comedy figures by appearing frayed, but "classy" in their dress suits, canes and gloves.

Exaggerated use of costume originated the identities of many comedians who, without their peculiarly identifiable garb, would not have established their public image. Silent films, having to rely completely upon the visual message, gave birth to a number of comedians whose humor relied upon costume. No one could find humor in a group of men chasing people if they weren't dressed as the famous Keystone Cops. Harold Lloyd developed comedy with the simple props of horn-rimmed glasses and straw hat, becoming a kind of sweet but hapless "nebbish." Despite his fame, when he was off camera and no longer wearing those well-known glasses and hat, he was unrecognizable to his thousands of fans. The same held true for the musical comedy comedian Bobby Clark who painted eyeglasses on his face with an eyebrow pencil, without which he would have been unnoticed and unfunny.

Hats for Comic Identity

The type of hat worn conceived many comedic characters other than Charlie Chaplin and Chico and Harpo Marx. Ed Wynn had his firechief's hat; Laurel and Hardy their bowler hats. In the television series of "The Honeymooners," Art Carney's character, Ed Norton, never parted with his battered felt hat perpetually pushed back from his forehead. Jackie Gleason's Reggie Van Gleason was pseudo-elegant in his topper. Minnie Pearl's entire image reflected her hat, with price tag attached. Jimmy Durante, playing and singing at the piano, always wore a battered fedora as much a part of him as his large nose and his "inka, dinka, doo."

Expressive Use of Costume

Expert, imaginative use of a costume can stir up comedy in diversified ways. In a particular production of Noël Coward's *Blithe Spirit*, the actress playing the role of Madame Arcati wore a calf-length black satin sheath which had a spiral of black silk

74

fringe beginning at the waist. While she was preparing herself for her communication with the spirit world, the actress shook the fringe as she bent her knees, increasing the tempo beat of the fringe as she went deeper into her trance; when the spirit arrived, the fringe became blissfully quiet. This actress learned the trick of engendering comedy by employing her costume expressively.

Beatrice Lillie

Beatrice Lillie had the knack of using the unexpected in a costume or prop to stimulate an audience's laughter. After singing a serious ballad in a lovely long evening gown, she'd raise her skirt and go gliding off stage on a pair of roller skates.

Carol Burnett

Through the course of all her television shows, Carol Burnett spawned a range of comic characters instantly recognizable by their costumes. Beginning with her own image, which she contrasted with a following series of costumes, she evolved into a nagging wife-daughter, a myriad of parodies of movie celebrities and their foibles, culminating in an endearing cleaning lady. Each personality was fashioned by overdone clothing cleverly achieved by knowledgeable use of wigs and costumes.

Even costumes themselves can become thoroughly identified with a particular role. Before copyright restrictions expired in 1964, it was a hard, fast rule that whoever played the lead in Brandon Thomas' *Charlie's Aunt* was required to wear the exact style dress in every performance as it was originally designed no matter who the actor may have been or what new idea he or the director may have had. Can you imagine Superman without his cape and tights? Clark Kent discovered immediately that he could not be identified as Superman and perform Superman feats unless he wore them.

Performers Inseparable From Their Costumes

Costume identities are not confined solely to comedians. The French singer and actor Maurice Chevalier performed together with his hard straw hat, creating the image of a jaunty boulevardier. Ted Lewis singing "Me and My Shadow" effectively created a memorable silhouette with his top hat. Liberace was among the first of the performers to wear particularly flamboyant clothing,

75

and his elaborately jeweled suits were just as much a part of his showmanship as his piano playing. From Elvis Presley to today's rock stars, all are identified with the clothing they wear in performance, and their performances are influenced by their clothing. Ronee Blakley, speaking of her role in Robert Altman's *Nashville*, said that once she got into her Barbara Jean wig and dress, no matter how she tried, she could speak only in the manner of Barbara Jean. And so it is not only for the serious actor, but the comedian, the singer, and the general overall entertainer whose costume becomes a part of him and his performance.

In the past actors dressed in extravagant, flamboyant style off-stage and off-screen, always playing the role of actor in public in order to set themselves apart from the everyday world of the general public. The public, in turn, has always been influenced by the clothing of performers and follow the fashions they have set.

Actors, Costumes and Fashion

When John Barrymore was the idol of the day, the type of collar he wore became the fashionable "Barrymore collar." A Joan Crawford movie introduced her "Letty Lynton sleeves," and a new fashion was born. Large, padded shoulders became another Joan Crawford hallmark to become generally adopted. From Elvis Presley's duck-tailed hair style and unique clothing to all the succeeding rock stars, their individual identities made imprints upon fashion, with the public striving for a resemblance to the performers. Each in her own time, the world has been filled with imitation Marilyn Monroes and Joan Crawfords, and presently there is increased theatricality in everyday dress.

There has to be a spark between the actor and the audience. It cannot be ignited unless there is a chemistry between the actor and the character he is playing. The identifying costume is a necessary component of that chemistry.

Chapter 10
MODES IN MIME

The alchemy of the actor is generated by his ability to instill his imagination into that of the audience. We have discussed the manner in which a costume's colors, fabrics, its message of time, place and manner, together with the actor's correct use, accords re-creation and re-enactment of reality. We have demonstrated the manner in which the costume can be distorted so that it becomes comedic. Distortion is one of the innovative uses of costume.

Innovational costuming undertaken by a performer provides an inspirational step forward to new directions. All facets of costume feed our fantasies and fever our ingenuity. Whatever we observe, use or possess has been discovered through imagination and improvisation. Implementing the costume with those two precious assets leads us straight to the door of illusion. Let's open it and discover the magic beyond.

The Bible tells us that "first there was the Word." Although we have no desire to dispute our beginnings, we assume language developed gradually. Conjuring the image of the first people on Earth, in order to make themselves understood and for the necessity of their survival, we see them discovering and improvising motions and gestures while making gutteral sounds.

Gesture alone, as in spoken language, requires interpretation. In the world of raw nature, to clarify message in motion, its bearer relied upon his surroundings. The branches and leaves of trees, rocks, colorful feathers of birds, skins of animals, were the devices he used to attempt communication and transmit his intentions. With a kind of intuitive certainty, we can believe that this method of explicitness provided the first improvised props and costumes.

Then came the Word. After its arrival, there arose a confusion of tongues, and man continued to rely upon motion and material to communicate. Mime and costume became the universal language.

The need for entertainment is a necessary diversion from the demands of existence. If reason tells us that mime was the genesis of communication, it consequently became the logical form of the early theatre. Natural mimics of motion, all people submit to its allure in music and dance; all people find kinship in the stories of others. Those with the talent to present them as artistic creations in mime formed the basis for all the theatrical arts that followed, elucidating and enhancing them with costume.

By the time mime was known as part of factual theatrical history, it was flourishing in religious practices, dressed in robes of ritual. The efficacy of its portrayal in the sacred and the profane depended then, as now, upon the ability of the performer to invent and utilize costume with proficiency.

Mime is performed in all countries and civilizations. Mime survives in legitimate theatre and film. Mime is the shape of juggling, acrobatics and dance. Mime discloses comedy and tragedy, good and evil. Executed ensemble or individually, its profusion of diversity overlaps every pattern of performance. Each of its manifold shapes bears a recognizable prototype of costume.

Commedia Dell'arte

When *commedia dell'arte* arrived on the scene, it gave off sparks that fired artists forever after. It enflamed pictorial arts, musical composers, dance choreographers, and every enactor of the performing arts. It also was the great-great grandfather of the stock character in the stock company.

Audiences visited old friends when they attended a *commedia* performance, knowing in advance that the villain would be foiled and deserved it, and that the hero and heroine, no matter what trickery they resorted to, would be happily rewarded. They didn't have to wait, either, to recognize each character, for the costume made the announcement immediately, and by that identification they knew what he'd be up to.

When capped and masked Harlequin appeared on-stage in his brilliantly colored diamond-patched costume and wooden sword, the spectators were certain he would save the day, by fair means or foul. He was their hero, who would overcome every obstacle and find a way, and however he did it, that was fine.

Perky Columbine, in her white, full-skirted dress, was always the ready companion to a love affair and intrigue. As the heroine, her actions were anticipated, and heartily endorsed.

Pantaloon, a skinny, crotchety old man, wore a hook-nosed mask with spectacles and was outfitted with a tight-fitting shirt and trousers and turned-up-at-the-toe slippers, all accentuating his skin-flintedness ways. More devoted to his wallet than wife or daughter, talkative and trusting, he was a natural to be cheated out of either one of them. Pantaloon was a deserving dupe and official fool. The audiences were delighted to see him outwitted again and again.

Gentle Pierrot with whitened face, a white, loose tunic and full trousers and cap enhanced his youth and poetic nature. Worthy of a part in any intrigue, advanced so the heroine would end up in his arms, his sweet pathos melted the spectators. All their sympathies resided in that charming lover.

It would appear difficult for an actor to achieve individuality in set characters and parts, but it is not likely that all actors accepted such anonymity. More probably, there were audiences' favorite players who could be distinguished by the little twists and turns they injected. No doubt there was a Harlequin whose by-play with stick and cap captivated onlookers. Or a Columbine, for flirtatious purposes, flipped her skirt with style, and with her charming ways acquired a following.

No Pierrot would sit by and watch this happen all around him without taking advantage of using the grace of his costume to make himself all the more romantic to the ladies of the audience. Pantaloon, refusing to be outdone by all this ingenious display, was not going to be tricked out of the effect of his on-stage gullibilities. He invented a few more clever uses for his turned-up slippers.

There were many more stock characters to round out the cast and fill in the action of the play — figures that joined the major ones adopted and adapted by their posterity for performances of their own.

The plays were not done in pantomime. Full of action, they had dialog and music, and all the improvisations of the players. These major personalities gave birth to a vast progeny. The advantage these offspring of the *commedia* had was the freedom to take their ancestors' basic form, and then improvise their costumes and movements. Performers, each changing the traditional costume to fit his ideas, received a great opportunity of individual expressiveness. Without inventive variations in costume, none of the exponents of the art of mime could have achieved his form, fame or individuality.

The *commedia dell'arte* troupes wandered through Italy, and eventually worked their way northward to France and England. In London, when the eighteenth century was relatively young, something new occurred in the *commedia*.

John Rich

John Rich was an actor, but he did not have the distinguishing advantage of a compelling voice. He owned a theatre in which he presented plays in pantomime featuring Harlequin, casting himself in the role. Pantomime was not entirely new to England, but it was given a different name: the Dumb Show. An example of it is to be found in Shakespeare's *Hamlet* at the point of Hamlet's encounter with a company of wandering players. At his invitation and direction they present their dumb show to inform Hamlet's mother and uncle, without the use of words, that he had knowledge of their guilt.

Neither was mime new. But it was John Rich, using the stage name of Lun, who launched and popularized it in England. Mime became universally set on its way.

Mime and Pantomime

There is a difference between mime and pantomime. Mime is exactly what the word implies: it mimics. Pantomime is telling a story without words. Both require the basic skills of mime.

The world is filled with mimes. As you walk along the streets of New York, San Francisco and other cities everywhere, you will see street mimes performing in traditional white-faced make-up, darkened eyebrows, darkly outlined eyes. Dressed in completely black or white leotards and tights, or a closely similar version of costume, it is difficult to distinguish one from the other. Mime is not an easy art to master, and to make it outstanding is even more challenging. Mime puts a burden upon the audience, for if it is not explicitly executed, and spectators cannot grasp it, the eventual effect is boredom and inattention. What is the solution?

Charlie Chaplin found it. He used imagination, innovation, improvisation and gradually developed an individuality. He is a direct descendent of Harlequin/Pierrot, but he had the creativity to modify the traditional costume and made it uniquely his own.

Assuming that your mimetic talent is finely honed and polished, you must have a distinguishing identity. One black and white figure among many of the same kind is as individual as one black bird, dove or penguin among twenty.

Marcel Marceau

Marcel Marceau is a classic mimic with surpassing talent, able to communicate with a minimum of props, yet presents a distinctive and recognizable figure. He remains a visual offspring of Pierrot, but we know him as Bip. How has he achieved this? Through his costume — subtle, effective, memorable. Look closely and you will see a stylized version of a French sailor. Under a closely cropped black jacket with three buttons on either side, is a horizontally-striped black and white dickey. The white trousers are bell-bottomed. A red, gauzy flower is attached to a battered black top hat set atop full black hair and wide sideburns. Sometimes the jacket is white, creating a full-fledged Pierrot appearance, with a touch of a mimic of Harlequin — but it's Bip.

Singular Identities

A solo performer in a distinctly individual art has tremendous advantage. He possesses the leeway and latitude of his imagination and inventiveness. And if you are artist enough to be a mimic, you have the creativity to establish a singular identity. No one can tell you what it should be, for true creation is an original act that cannot be taught. It involves daydreams and practical practice, fantasies and experiments, trying, scrapping it all, then trying again. That is the manner in which Charlie Chaplin evolved his Tramp, and Red Skelton gave life to a series of characters with the deft crushing of a hat.

Chaplin, Marceau, Skelton: three people of classic mime each discovered his own way to rise above uniformity. And once you have found your own individual personality, it will take you anywhere you allow it to lead.

Joseph Grimaldi

Joseph Grimaldi was another mime who took his own innovative turn, and introduced and refined the art of the clown. Grimaldi easily developed his skill with the heritage his father passed on to him. The elder Grimaldi was an entertainer at the fairgrounds he owned in France. Taken to London as a boy, young Grimaldi performed and danced at Sadler's Wells Varieties, excelling in pantomime. His understanding of the joys of uninhibited entertainment made it a natural step to developing the *commedia dell'arte* buffoon Punchinello as the model for his clown.

Punchinello was short, fat, hook-nosed and hunchbacked. A tall, pointed hat on his head, he wore a loose blouse and his baggy pants covered a huge belly. On this basic character, Grimaldi, master of pantomime, generated a clown with as many costumes as his imagination would permit, combining them with ingenious props, turned them into devices for laughter. From cheeses to coal scuttles to vegetables, and from luridly colored jester's attire to ludicrous uniforms and jingling bells — every object and outlandishly clever costume became the tools of his technique. His innovations became deeply imbedded into his own identity, so that even in his retirement from the stage he could not easily separate himself from costume.

Holding fast to Grimaldi as the ideal, other clowns followed. Such an entertaining clown naturally found his home in the circus, and forever after the circus could not exist without him. Some clowns became famous, others perhaps did not achieve particular note. But their unique costumes and antics each delighted generations of children who grew up with memories that drew them back to the circus with their own children.

Clowns of Many Characters

Clowns belong to countries of divergent cultures. Clown is a worldwide performer, at home everywhere. His popularity is based upon his ability to create laughter through the *appearance and use of his costume.*

Clown has two faces: either he creates a character who is completely comedic, or, since comedy and tragedy have but a slender thread between them, he chooses to be a laughter-through-tears performer. To be a clown is an opportunity of greatest freedom in forming a character. It allows for unlimited individuality with no restrictions except to provide comedy or the subtlety of comedy blended with pathos.

The clown is the symbol of theatre's two masks of comedy and tragedy. Within these choices are categories of assorted images and types of clowns, and you have the singular opportunity to determine what you feel is personally suitable. Something within your own personality and character will automatically make the decision for you:

Perhaps you have a physical appearance that almost dictates the sort of clown you will be. Do you have bowed legs? A large nose? A body exceptionally tall and thin? An elongated face? Accentuate your singularity and build your costume around it.

Your natural inclinations and outlook could possibly lead you toward the sad clown. You see humor in life's frustrations, and follow your compulsion to develop that aspect in your act and appearance.

You may observe a person in the street who has a peculiar walk, mannerism or appearance that strikes you as being so humorous, you are inspired to develop a clown in his image. Your mind leaps to all the absurd possibilities that can be enhanced and utilized by a costume emphasizing that oddity.

In a shop you spot a particular type of clothing that strikes you as ridiculous. It provokes the conception and birth of a droll and ludicrous eccentric who will become immediately identified in a costume provoked by your observance.

You are influenced by preceding clowns of certain tradition but develop an adaptation of costume and performance appropriate to your own talents and perceptions.

Whatever inspiration leads you to your preference, your first step is to decide how you are going to accentuate it *together with your make-up and costume*, for that is the crux of your clown's personality. Your total appearance must emphasize it. Concentrate first upon your make-up, experimenting until you have invented a distinctive face prompted by your clown's peculiarities and actions. Then choose your color or combination of colors. Your selection is of utmost importance. Re-read the section in this book referring to color and its various effects upon emotion and visual effect (Chapter 5) to determine what is suitable to the nature of your clown.

Following that, carefully examine and analyze all of your actions in performance since your costume is much more than your appearance; it is your assistant in performance. You may be executing tricks that will use parts of your costume, and you will therefore build your costume around those stunts. You might choose to hide an arm under your costume and have a stuffed, fake one attached to your shoulder by Velcro and covered by the sleeve. Offer that arm to shake hands with a member of your audience, and it comes off in his hand. This illustration of a trick that surprises and amuses is solely devised by your costume. As it gradually takes shape, work with the outfit so that not only will it conform to what you want it to do, remembering to keep it comfortable and workable as you go along, it will serve as an instigator for further expansion of your act.

Each one sees a clown in his own way. The film director, Frederico Fellini, was fascinated by them from childhood and figured them in some of his films. For him they were symbolic. He did not see them in color, but exclusively in black or white.

He viewed the white clown as the representative of high principles, wisdom and beauty but concerned with his public image. His arrogant eyebrows and a harsh mouth were accentuated by a whitened face. The black clown of Fellini's conception is the tramp who tries, but for whom circumstances never improve. We are reminded of Chaplin. Color plays the major role in these visualizations: stark black or white.

The Russian clown, Oleg Popov, regarded his own brain child as an ordinary, cheerful chap, tender of heart, with a touch of the poet. He did not want him in the traditional bright, flamboyant colors. Like Fellini, he saw the clowns in terms of black and white, but joined as one. He combined the colors in a costume consisting of a black and white checked cap, black caftan-type of suit, white shirt and black ribbon around the neck. He offset the black and white effect with hair the color of straw. In agreement with Fellini as to color, the likeness was not in accord. He established his unique idea and matched it to the costume.

Each performer has the right to his own perception, make-up and attire. Emmett Kelly identified and emphasized the sad nature of his clown by painting full lips in an exaggerated downward position, a tear upon his cheek.

Suited to history and place, clowns have infinite faces and costumes. As jesters in the royal courts, there to amuse kings, queens, lords and ladies, they wore long peaked caps topped with jingling bells, or attached donkey ears, or any other unflattering prop to give them the appearance of complete fools. They were amusing and witty, and many jesters took advantage of their position to say and do what others dared not. Even if their words were offensive, foolish costumes protected them and belied their mockery.

Circus Clowns

But when we think of clowns, we usually associate them with the circus. Sometimes, if there is a large spectacle with a particular theme in mind, designers conceive the costumes. At all times the circus clown is responsible for his make-up and most often his own costume design. The ruff or collar is part of the history of the clown and synonymous with the classic notion, but not always used.

Among the circus clowns the prevailing mood is one of joyousness and frivolity. One Barnum and Bailey clown was especially ingenious in his costume. Working in tandem with a midget, he dressed himself as a funny, fat lady. The midget was attached onto his back, as part of the clown's bustle. The clown walked forward, swaying under his exaggerated costume. He would lose his bustle. The dropped bustle then ran behind, trying to catch up with the clown.

It is not unusual for clowns to work in such pairs, and it is under these circumstances that costume plays an especially amusing and clever part. Not only do clowns work with other people, they work with animals, who are also in costume. And don't think

Clown with midget inside bustle.

that the animals are not just as responsive to costume as the clown in performing the act. Haven't you seen a monkey in dress and bonnet, waddling along, deliberately preening himself? What about the elephant who seems to take delight in sitting on a stool in his skirt and ruffles around his ankles? And dogs, standing on their hind legs, mincing around in their frilly costumes? Who isn't impressed by handsomely adorned horses, proudly prancing around the ring? Every creature responds to costume. When the clown works with a partner or an animal he has another novelty in costume to invent to function jointly with his own. It takes experimentation and working with the results before there is a final determination.

A clown has wondrous fabrics with which to fashion his costume — bright, varied colors in a profusion of fabric varieties, and materials that glow in the dark — a magical mélange to excite and stir the imagination.

Television Clowns

Performing clowns include both men and women. Not all clowns appear on stage or in the circus, nor do they assume only one identity or style. Television had its own remarkable clown in Lucille Ball. Her fanciful antics were boundless. Dressed in a tail-coat she became a performing seal; in an Italian peasant dress and scarf, she was in a huge vat stamping grapes into wine. Another episode produced a Lucy dressed as a Ziegfeld girl balancing an enormous headdress. As she walked down the long flight of stairs, she struggled to hang on to that cumbersome headdress until she finally lost it. As it tumbled down the stairs, she froze in the middle of the staircase, a totally bereft expression upon her face.

Harpo Marx, whose wooly wig and hat became an extension of himself and gave him a never-to-be-forgotten identity, appeared on Lucy's show. Lucy, dressed in identical Harpo attire, stood opposite him. Together they performed pantomimed pranks in mirror image. She was continually resourceful, shrewd in her selection of costumes, adept in comporting herself with them to create hilarious situations.

In the days before coming events were widely promoted through newspapers, magazines, radio and television, the only way folks knew that a circus was coming to town was with the arrival of an advance man. He was usually one of the clowns. Making his announcement on an improvised platform, he presented the gathering with a small foretaste of what awaited, performing antics and teasing the crowd. Then came the circus parade! Pouring into town in a stream of gaudy caravans and ornamented elephants, zany clowns waved and tooted horns, acrobats tumbled, fire-eaters amazed, equestriennes in their pink skirts led the handsomely decorated horses, the brass band thrilled. Flashing colors and costumes spontaneously played to the crowd — and everyone's heart beat fast with excitement.

Mime, Costumes and Parades

One of the most joyful and spectacular displays of mime and costume and improvisation is the parade. It is part of America's heritage. When a drama or musical show made its entrance in town, it was preceded by a costumed procession of actors. Thus was born the Mummers' Parade. Cherished and perpetuated in Philadelphia, every New Year's Day it comes to life once again. Men are clothed in dazzlingly beautiful women's gowns. Others are adorned with life-like duplications of birds, their bodies bedecked with enormous feathered fantails, disguised as and strutting with the pride of peacocks. String bands accompany the parade, some musicians adorned in satins that are spangled and feathered, and others in metallic cloth of gold and silver that gleam in the sunlight. Inspired by the color and representation of his costume, each mummer moves according to his own impulses to enhance his appearance and please the fascinated onlookers.

Still another parade of tradition, costume, mime and invention is the New Orleans Mardi Gras, planned by individual clubs, each with its own leader, all devoting time continually throughout the year to the preparation of costumes which will disguise them and give them freedom to act as they wish. It culminates in the lighthearted parade headed by the King and Queen of Mardi Gras.

The Pasadena Parade of Roses is a yearly event. Thousands of fresh flowers decorate ingeniously constructed costumes and floats, each forming a theatre upon which their participants are affected by the distinctive beauty of the magnificent spectacle they developed with care and pride, and the approbation of the spectators.

And the most American parades of all: the ethnic parades of the Irish, Polish, German, Hungarian, Chinese, Japanese, and all other Americans of various lineage who display in typical movement and dance the costumes of their heritage.

It is mime. It is improvisation. It is costume.

Mime and Pantomime in Silent Films

Mime and pantomime coherently expressed through costume do not reside exclusively within the realm of comic and seriocomic. While silent film nurtured and produced mimes and comedians whose genius and talents fortunately are permanently recorded and available to be admired and perhaps emulated, there were other performers whose skill in costumed pantomime granted them their prominence in silent film.

The ability to convey a story without words, and the gift to establish distinctive and dissimilar characters in a variety of stories, was the major accomplishment of the film actors of the silent screen era. Since the people they portrayed could not be identified by spoken dialog, the costumes they wore, combined with pantomimed action, told the tale with clarity.

Lon Chaney

The most compelling mime, actor, costume and make-up expert in silent films was Lon Chaney. As the son of parents who were deaf mutes, mime became the language between parents and child. In order to communicate with them he learned the movements of expression with every portion of his body as thoroughly as one acquires a spoken language. No one could be more suited to arouse emotion in silence than Lon Chaney, and his extraordinary innovations of costume and make-up earned him a title that no one could ever usurp: the Man of a Thousand Faces.

Among his enduring roles was his appearance as a clown in both *He Who Gets Slapped* and *Laugh, Clown, Laugh*. Each a comic-tragic clown, they were traditional in costume and make-up, but his poignant interpretation of them rendered them unforgettable. The vast number of personalities he developed with costume and make-up almost obliterated his clowns by placing them in the shadow of portrayals that endure as monuments of an actor's supreme accomplishments.

The mastery of his thousand faces rested not only in his extraordinary ability to create them, but to adopt posture and attitude as compelling as make-up and costume. He worked diligently to use them as the foundation to form emotional facets of the character. He observed how people dressed and moved, then he recreated them with the essence of absolute reality. He knew that attire and body movement were more indicative of the inner core of an individual than his speech. His range of convincing and mesmerizing personalities continued beyond *The Hunchback of Notre Dame* and *The Phantom of the Opera*. In those he was ugly but

89

appealing in his pathos. With a minimum of make-up, relying solely upon costume, his renditions of a Russian peasant and a Marine sergeant were equally convincing as he imparted with truth the emotional qualities of the inner person. His tools were observance, imagination, innovation, and dedication. No performer will be convincing and compelling without them.

Lon Chaney in The Hunchback of Notre Dame.

One of the preeminent people in this new industry to recognize Lon Chaney's abilities was William S. Hart, famous as one of movie's leading cowboys. Hart's prior experience was in theatre. He appeared in Shakespearean roles and noted for his part as Messala, the villain, in a Broadway production of *Ben-Hur*. He had been far removed from the silent cowboy and his horse, but his western outfit recast his acting career.

The Quiet "Western"

The Western became one of the most popular forms of film. It was a perfect vehicle for action without words. Giving an actor a ten-gallon hat, jacket, neckerchief, cowboy boots, a white hat if he was a "good guy," a black hat for the troublemakers, equipping him with holster and gun, movie directors spawned a cowboy striding and riding macho-style all over the screen. In such a combination of clothing, the actor had no choice but to be virile, tough and a straight-shooter. Dressing a number of other actors in feathered headdresses, beads, moccasins, then providing them with bow and arrow, American Indians were silently stealing all over the place, or whooping it up with a mute battle cry. All this, without a sound, kept audiences either anxious or triumphant. Without those costumes, no actor could have begun to be a cowboy or Indian.

Not all was high drama, touching moments, the wild west, and accomplished actors. The silent film was not heavily populated with skilled actors. Many had never performed before. But the perspicacious producers of early film had the aptitude to recognize appealing individuals who possessed adaptability and susceptibility to suggestion.

Heavy-breathing romance was another lure to the movie theatre. Attractive but unseasoned, two people emerged as exponents of the art of seduction.

Theda Bara

High on the temptation list was Theda Bara. Privately, she was intelligent and reserved in manner. Publicly, she became the dangerous vampire-like woman. Her ordinary name was replaced by an anagram for "death" and "Arab." Inexperienced in acting, barely concealed in low-cut, clinging gowns or diaphanous veiling, she converted herself into a woman men secretly longed for but feared for her dangerous ensnarements. Theda Bara achieved adeptness in dramatizing her enticing clothing, developed a much-imitated writhing, sensually wrapped walk, acquired her designation as "the Vamp," and became the epitome of allure.

Rudolph Valentino

Among silent film's romantic heroes, Rudolph Valentino was the most adored. With assets limited to proficiency in dance and a handsome face, his costumes and commitment developed his endowments. Although he was most famous for his role as an Arab sheik in turban and robe, he carried himself with authenticity in

The Museum of Modern Art Film Stills Archive 1 W. 53rd. Street, New York City

Rudolph Valentino in The Sheik

the eighteenth-century attire of Monsieur Beaucaire. As a proud
bullfighter in *Blood and Sand*, and in every role he undertook,
he orchestrated his dancer's grace with costume and pantomimed
action, and became a legendary actor.

Rudolph Valentino in Monsieur Beaucaire

93

With emphasis upon personality and appearance, each star was distinctly recognizable and identified by his raiment and make-up of a specific role. The clothing not only changed the actor's appearance, it became the ally to a coherent performance.

Many times, in those play-it-by-ear days, with only an outline for a script, it was improvisation all the way. Everyone arrived with no experience in this new medium. Those who acted on the stage had the prior advantage of the spoken word. On the screen, motion and costume were all they possessed. There was no other means of portrayal. The costume had to be ingeniously cultivated to vividly depict the character's personality. It was absolutely necessary for the actor to enterprisingly avail himself of its assistance in action, conveyance of meaning and rendering of emotion. It was his voice and instrument.

Silent films became the universal entertainment. Whatever language was spoken in any region of the world where they were seen, each viewer understood the emotions and action without the necessity of subtitles. The actors and their costumes became historic monuments. These great stars of the silver screen remain shining in filmdom heaven.

Mime and Dance

The blending of motion, rhythm and space combine to create a striking form of mime: dance. Color and costume with its supplementary parts are the stimuli for continual reshaping of dance form. Without music, dance becomes an aesthetic exercise; without costume, dance is neither enlivened nor significant. Dance is old and primitive; dance is new and modern; in performance it has always worn a formative disguise. Music and dance radiate emotion heightened and intensified by costume.

Dance in performance has become one of our liveliest arts. When audiences first encountered it as primarily limited to classic ballet, its appeal was narrow. Innovative dancing choreographers made it inviting to large numbers. Each discovered costume to be an integral part of inventiveness.

Rooted in Columbine, the ballerina in her pink toe shoes and tutu symbolizes the traditional form of classic ballet. To be original and creative is to become free of tradition, and the origins of modern dance began with the shedding of the tutu.

94

Michel Fokine

Michel Fokine was the revolutionary of Russian ballet. His *Les Sylphides* reshaped the ritual patterns of ballet movement and ballerina tutus were replaced by long, gossamer skirts. These delicately graceful skirts emphasized the softening of the dancer's arm movements and the rigidity of the ballet began to melt.

Loie Fuller

This revolution was fomented in the United States by Loie Fuller. Rotund of figure, conforming to the general shape of women's bodies of the late nineteenth century, and with none of the requisite abilities of a dancer except for her arm movements, she discovered that extraordinary effects could be rendered with a length of sheer silk. She progressed to the intricate manipulation of huge, brilliantly colored skirts and transformed them into delicate flowers or riotous flames. She comprehended all the possibilities of light and color, placed lanterns upon the stage that threw off spectrum colors upon her swirling, twirling skirts, metamorphosing them into recognizable shapes or fascinating designs. Dancing with a large white scarf, she culminated the dance by working the scarf into a lily. Covered by an ample gown of delicate fabric, she concealed sticks under gigantic sleeves and shaped herself into the appearance of a butterfly. She dubbed her intricate movements with costume, color and light "The Serpentine" dance, and became America's sensational dancer of the nineteenth century's last decade.

With constraints of formality abolished, and dramatic use of costume and color established, a chain reaction set in and innovative dance was set on its course.

Isadora Duncan

Isadora Duncan became the next exponent of this new freedom. Fascinated by classical Greek figures, she veiled herself in flowing diaphanous robes and uninhibitedly danced barefooted throughout Europe, promulgating her belief in the freedom of spirit and body movement. Freedom is infectious, and upon seeing Duncan perform in Russia, Fokine carried this reformation of dance with him to Paris.

Vaslav Nijinsky

Imbued with the zest of change, Fokine the choreographer, Sergei Diaghilev the producer, and Léon Bakst the designer, put another link into the chain of innovative dance and costume, and expressed it through Vaslav Nijinsky.

Nijinsky fascinated and astounded spectators with his complete absorption into his roles. He recognized that his absolute identification with the part depended upon the costume and his rites of performance centered upon it. First, he studied the costume designs, and, after meeting his meticulous approval, insisted they be exactly executed as sketched. He approached his costume with complete knowledge of its link with the choreography, and that he could not be transported into the essence of the role without a covering disguise.

Those within his intimate circle were familiar with his preparations before a performance. He began by warming up in practice clothes alone at the back of the stage, then freshening himself prior to a half-hour devoted to applying his own make-up. Through it all, his languid manner persisted. Then the enchantment began. As he gradually changed his clothing, he appeared tense and impulsive. Once in costume, another personality imperceptibly emerged, and as he gazed at himself in the mirror, it appeared to onlookers that his entire being entered into this new entity by which he seemed to have been overtaken. His costume bewitched him; he bewitched his audience.

Ruth St. Denis

Back in the United States another link in innovative dance was forged by Ruth St. Denis. Following the path we suggest all performers to take, she researched libraries and museums in pursuit of the exotic customs, costumes and dances of Egypt, the Orient and India. The early twentieth-century public was fascinated by foreign and unusual displays of costume and dance since few could ever see them anywhere but upon the stage.

As East Indian Goddess Rhada, glorified in a swirling golden skirt, a jacket beaded with coral and turquoise, bracelets encircling her arms and tinkling bells upon her fingers, bared legs and middle in what was then shocking display, she brought all the alluring lore of India into her dance and the view of the audience. Introducing more of the foreign fascinations of India, in somber brown costume, she became a snake charmer, green rings upon her fingers manipulated to represent cobra's eyes, her arms the snake. A full range of color and costume became incorporated into her dance.

Ted Shawn

Innovative in creating his own handsomely costumed Spanish and assorted ethnic dances, Ted Shawn became the first man prominently figured in American dance. In him, Ruth St. Denis found the perfect mate and partner. Together they formed Denishawn, and through their school of dance united with costume, the chain of modern dance grew longer and stronger with links of their increasingly imaginative adaptations of alien attire. Martha Graham became a student of Denishawn, a member of their troupe, and ultimately a teacher.

Martha Graham

When Martha Graham left Denishawn, she retreated from the colorful garb and dances of exotic lands. Native America and its primal austerities initially inspired Graham, which she delineated by movement, costume and color. Her unique simplification of costume emphasized beauty of movement, and tubular jerseys became part of her perceptions. The stretching jersey encasing her writhing body magnified the grief of "Lamentation." At all times her costumes were expressions of movement and emotion. Lengthy cuts of fabric, capes and color assumed symbolic meanings. She used leotards imaginatively: by attaching a circular skirt at the back waist of a leotard and drawing it to the front, then wrapping the upper legs with the skirt, she achieved an effective result. Contouring abstract figures in dance at the same

97

time artists were inventing their abstractions on canvas, Martha Graham recast movement, meaning and emotion with costume and color.

Established as the doyenne of modern dance, others reinterpreted Martha Graham or advanced their own concepts. Leotard and tights became the basic uniform of professional dancers, to be embellished in accordance with individual insights.

Vernon and Irene Castle

American audiences were inundated with abundant forms of dance, and welcomed them all. Vernon and Irene Castle introduced ballroom dancing as an entertainment with their famous Castle Walk, and the public put on their best clothes and devoted themselves to mastering the popular dances that began to proliferate. Spanish costumes romanticized the tango and a new craze was born. Diaghilev's company arrived with Nijinsky and its spectacularly artistic sets and costumes. Admiration for ballet surged, and Anna Pavlova later became the heralded ballerina.

Thrills of the dance world seemed unending. Léonide Massine brought his exciting *Gaieté Parisienne* and its exhilarating cancan dance, the dancers abandoning themselves into the wild joy of the music and the flashing, alluring colors of their skirts.

Elegant Costumes for Dancers

Elegance in dress brought a new phase of dance: the artistic exhibition ballroom dance team of two. Smoothly combed gentlemen, meticulously dressed in formal attire of black tie, brilliantly white shirts, set off with handsome cuff links gleaming below sleeves of black tail-coated jackets topping sharply creased trousers, exemplified the requisite standards for expert ballroom dancing. Their women partners, hair drawn away from their faces and elegantly knotted behind their sleek, graceful heads, were gowned in flowing chiffons, embellished with floating scarves, luxurious feathers, beaded and sequined skirts full and fluid, pleated or fringed, swaying and swirling with the rhythm of the dance. The colors were either exciting or romantic and subdued, reflecting the music. It was the Age of the Sophisticated Lady and elegant supper clubs, of the chanteuse, each enveloped in clothing to enhance beauty, grace and chic. Famous dancing pairs shaped their individualities through dance technique and their manner of dress: Veloz and Yolande and Tony and Renee De Marco on stage; Fred Astaire and Ginger Rogers on film.

Ballroom dancing and its exquisite attire gave more than pleasure to the spectator. It sent America to the dance floor. To go dancing meant to put on one's prettiest dress or most handsome suit. Each person wore a carefully selected costume and went dancing. When youthful America discovered the jitterbug, the required uniform for the girls was a swinging skirt and a pair of saddle shoes. Disco dancing established its own dress and flashing lights. The world became a dancing stage, and the performers arrived in appropriate attire.

Costumes for Ballet

George Balanchine drew his ballets from the sound of music and colored them with costumes, and was the first to integrate classical ballet with the Broadway musical. Balanchine conceived a spoof of the ballet *Schéhérazade* in Richard Rodgers and Lorenz Hart's *On Your Toes*. Then he gave the show a dramatic turn in *Slaughter On Tenth Avenue*, a sensual ballet enactment of a romance culminating in violence. The striking costumes worn by Tamara Geva and Ray Bolger, combined with Balanchine's electrifying choreography and their inspired performance, enkindled the extension of ballet into musical theatre.

Costumes for Musicals

Agnes de Mille followed suit and set a style in Rodgers and Hammerstein's *Oklahoma!* In a ballet dream sequence that advanced the story line, male dancers became cowboys and ballerinas were enticing dance hall girls. Ballet acquired an additional turn, and a new breed of choreographers made their stage entrance.

Costumes for Modern Dance

Modern dance progresses with original characterizations established solely with masks, or obliterations of the human figure reshaped into other images with the use of configurations of lights, properties and costume; there are always ceaselessly fresh innovations. Ballet continues with its own group of imaginative creators. Dance, as in all artistic quests, is ever changing, advancing ideas influenced by the past, shaped by current discoveries and forecasts of the future, always underscored and translated by costume and color.

Fanny Brice

In each era of taste and outlook, entertainers appear upon the scene to comment and assess the period, to see it from the viewpoint of humor and satire. Fanny Brice, a seriocomic performer who reflected the sophistication of her era in elegant dress and dramatic song, would turn that image upside down in costume. This "Funny Lady," in a feathered headdress, became a Jewish-American Indian; in a bathing suit, she was the caricature of a mother on the beach at Coney Island. Her performances were concurrent with the bombardment of all varieties of dance form, and she delivered her own dance commentary in mime. Encased in a long tube of jersey, she executed "artistic movements" until she was so tied up in knots, it became her inescapable trap. She attacked another form of dance. Arrayed in a tutu, teetering on toe shoes, in a unique form of obeisance to Anna Pavlova, she presented her comical dying swan in an outlandish version of the ballet *The Dying Swan.*

Mime in its multiplicity of modes presents individual portraits, each distinguished by the talent and viewpoint of the performer. The jersey tube and the traditional tutu worn by a dancer-mime become objects of beauty and meaning; worn by a comic-mime, they become objects of laughter. All depends upon the skill and ingenuity of the performer with his costume.

It is mime. It is innovation. It is costume.

Chapter 11
THE PUPPET MASTER

Imagination and novelty constitute the world of the puppeteer. He is a mysterious figure who endows the puppet with life, provides it with adventures, then extinguishes its existence. The puppet is completely at his mercy. The puppet master empowers us to accept unreality as actuality.

For all of its enchanting ways, the puppet is only a shape encased in a costume. The puppeteer gives it voice, but the costume is its life's blood, shaping its individuality and temperament.

The Beginning of Puppetry

Puppetry's first appearance is as indistinct as our own. The family tree of the performing arts has many branches, and its seeds may have been planted in early religious ceremonies throughout the world. History intimates that ventriloquism and puppetry mated during those rites, enabling Grecian, Roman and Oriental gods to speak through images. There is evidence that hollow tubes constructed within idols allowed a ventriloquist's words to pass through them and eminate from rigid lips. Forewarning, forecasting and threatening, these gods commanded awe and fear.

Puppets, substituting for human sacrifice, served as appeasers to demanding deities. They appeared in sacred medieval dramas garbed in the robes of revered religious figures, and performed in theatrical entertainments of ancient Greece and the Orient. One of those tiny glorified figures may have been tenderly referred to as "little Mary," and later became known as the marionette attached to her strings.

Just as the Old Testament forbade the worship of the idol, so did the Christian church eventually evict puppetry and ventriloquism from its sanctuary. Ventriloquism remained at home in less widely practiced religions where forms of witchcraft existed. The voodoo doll, often costumed in garments resembling those of victim or supplicant, was given a voice, and the local witch served as its puppet master.

Some puppets retained their dignity and continued to live on in their own theatres, enacting roles in religious presentations. Others presented legends and dramas, or branched out into performing Shakespearean plays. The strings attached to these full-bodied and jointed marionettes allowed them to move realistically. Dressed in the raiment of the characters they represented, they became puppet counterparts to the serious actor.

Street Puppetry

The remaining puppets, like outcast children, took to the streets. They enjoyed the vagabond life, became carnival figures, participated in street fairs and performed at fairgrounds. As often occurs with such associations, they developed into bawdy characters. In Italy they became acquainted with the crowd belonging to the *commedia dell'arte* and borrowed their acts. One of the puppets, who was a marionette, met Pulcinello, at times known as Punchinello, and adopted his name. When he migrated to England, he shortened it to Punch. There he married Judy.

Since he and Judy were part of the rough-and-tumble crowd, they moved with more facility as hand puppets. Each one of these figures was, in reality, formed by a rough, woolen cloth glove with a wooden head attached. Their sturdy, coarse costumes suited the life they led.

Punch resembled a court jester in his tall, pointed red and green cap, the tip of which curled downward by the weight of its tassel. The ruff around his neck did not distract from the fact that he was not a handsome fellow. Round buttons marching down his red jacket curved over a huge belly supported by the belt beneath it. Judy was conservatively dressed in

her long grey dress and mobcap. She was no beauty either, and as the years passed, as sometimes happens with husbands and wives, they resembled one another. Somewhere along the way, each had grown a large hooked nose.

No one knows with certainty anything about Judy's past, except that at times she used the name of Joan. Judy turned into a nagging wife who drove Punch to acts of mayhem. Punch and Judy established the comedic branch of the puppet family.

Punch's relative, Guignol, the French hand puppet, was a native of Lyon, and he naturally wore the clothing and had the appearance of his fellow townsmen who were weavers of silk. But the town couldn't contain him, and he went to Paris. He was a particularly amusing fellow, became a popular actor for whom many plays have been written, and a true Parisian.

Behind each of our historical puppets was its master. Perhaps the ventriloquist who spoke for the idol was a devout priest — or a cynic. A resourceful actor possibly preferred the novel choice of dramatic performances in puppet theatres. The carnival man behind Punch may have been an errant husband publicly expressing his marital woes. All became adept in costuming puppets to shape distinguishing characteristics.

It is difficult to think of these tiny, appealing figures in terms of a piece of wood, plastic, foam rubber, papier-mâché, or a glove. Yet, underneath the costume, that's all you'll find.

A Puppet Is a Costume

What is the puppet? It is a costume. And what is a costume? It is the immediate and accurate description of a character. Its color is the reflection of the puppet's mood and personality. Costume is the only identification the puppet possesses and the key to all he represents. The costume is the performer.

What propels this performer into action? The puppet master, of course, whose only means of molding the character of the puppet and his own performance is through the costume. The total actor is the costumed puppet and its manipulator. It is, indeed, "a most ingenious paradox."

For an actor, puppetry is the ultimate and absolute disguise. It provides him with unparalleled freedom of expression and originality. Although he has established the puppet's character through the costume and provides its voice and movement, he remains free of his own ego while expressing his individual ideas through the puppet. The puppet is his stand-in, and it is the puppet who bears the responsibility of the puppet master's words and actions.

The Puppeteer and the Ventriloquist

The two acts of puppetry and ventriloquism are allied. The animated doll is the similarity. The difference is the visibility or invisibility of the puppet master. Usually the puppeteer is hidden from public view and speaks only through the puppets, changing the quality and tone of his voice to suit the character. The ventriloquist is visible to the audience, placing his voice so that the sound seemingly emanates from the doll, with lips unmoving until he speaks for himself.

While puppetry propagated, ventriloquism went underground, eventually re-emerging as a form of disembodied entertainment. When it became heavily populated with performers presenting similar acts, some ventriloquists acquired a doll, known as a "familiar," or "figure." One of the most famous of figures was Edgar Bergen's dummy-doll, Charlie McCarthy.

Charlie was born during a period in American history that prized sophistication and wit. It was the time of elegant dress and clever repartee. Nightclubs were filled with finely dressed men and women, and luxuriously costumed performers. The *Esquire Magazine* became the bible and guide for the sartorial splendor of debonair gentlemen.

Edgar Bergen

Edgar Bergen fully grasped the tenor of the time. Both he and Charlie made their stage and movie appearances formally attired in top hat, white tie and tails. Charlie also wore a slightly sardonic smile, and a monocle over one of his large brown eyes. The team became famous on radio, where shows were performed before live audiences, explicit enough for the listening audience to create its own image of the performers.

Charlie McCarthy and Edgar Bergen.

Bergen and McCarthy possessed two distinct voices and characters: Bergen's soft and gentlemanly; McCarthy's brash and bold. Charlie was irreverent toward all the famous who were guest artists on the radio programs, making witty observations about the visitors, and expressing opinions that would normally remain unsaid except in privacy. Although they were identically dressed, his personality was so distinctly apart from Bergen's, whose role was to chastise Charlie for his outrageous speech and manner, it never occurred to anyone that this character was under Bergen's control. Bergen was regarded as obviously not responsible for Charlie's remarks and actions, and Charlie was disarmingly forgivable. They were accepted as two separate individuals.

105

Charlie McCarthy's photographs, which appeared in magazines and newspapers, recorded his meetings with presidents, prime ministers and movie stars. He was decorated by the King of Sweden, and met Eleanor Roosevelt. When Mrs. Roosevelt was introduced to him, she involuntarily extended her hand to shake his. Bergen seemed to be just a tagalong to this celebrity.

Bergen astutely created a personality in conformity with his dress. The formal attire gave Charlie an air of urbanity, wit and man about town, and the monocle endowed Charlie with an air of superiority over Bergen. Charlie could get away with anything.

Puppets for Television

Television provides an inviting medium for ventriloquists and puppeteers. Its reduced-in-size stage establishes an intimacy between puppets and audience. Shari Lewis's hand puppet, Lamb Chop of the downcast eyes and appealing face, was so charming a television personality, it was not apparent that she was only a ventriloquist's hand in a wooly lamb costume, for all eyes were on shy Lamb Chop — an adorable, cuddly animal. Shari Lewis's innovative mind bred an idea, shaped it into a costume, gave it a voice, and created a little lamb.

The talking hand became another puppet favorite. Señor Wences' Johnny was comprised of lips painted at the point where forefinger and thumb meet, eyes and nose painted above them on his bare hand, topped by a wig. Beneath the hand was the cloth body of a boy. Wences was inventive, and the television audience accepted Johnny as a delightful child.

Puppets and Children

Children have a natural affinity with puppets. Every child who plays with a doll or teddy bear treats it as a living creature. The child empathizes with dolls, for a young girl knows what it means to be a kind of combination plaything and object of adult direction. She is cuddled, kissed and bathed, told when to eat and sleep, reprimanded when she is naughty. Held by her arms as a marionette on strings, she learns to walk. She is given words to repeat. The child transfers her experiences to the doll, commands it in the way she has been commanded, looked after as she has been looked after. It is loved and cared for, spanked and scolded. The doll's clothes are part of important decisions, for when the doll is taken for a walk, or to a party, it is dressed to suit the occasion. At the end of the day, it must be undressed, diapered and put to bed. The doll assumes the role of her companion and comforter over which she retains control. Between them there is private conversation. The child becomes both puppet master and ventriloquist.

Howdy Doody

Television was in its own childhood when it fell in love with a doll. Bob Smith presided over a Saturday morning kiddie show on radio where he gave voice to a character whose cheerful greeting was "Howdy Doody"; the salutation became his name. Howdy Doody materialized into television's first puppet. He was a big-eared, wide-grinning, freckle-faced marionette, dressed in belted blue jeans, cowboy boots, plaid shirt and neckerchief. America's children adopted him as their own. Puppets found a home on television.

Kukla, Fran and Ollie

A major charm of puppetry is its air of spontaneity. Kukla, Fran and Ollie had it in abundance. While Burr Tillstrom was invisibly manipulating his hand puppet family, nonpuppet Fran Allison joined them out front for television visits. The easy manner and friendship between the puppets and an actual person gave the impression that, underneath the Kuklapolitans' costumes, living hearts were beating and their emotions were real.

Kukla was an endearing round-faced boy with a ball for a nose, and Ollie, a temperamental, nonconforming dragon. The Kuklapolitans were a large brood of lovable oddballs: zany Beulah Witch flew around on her broomstick; Madame Oglepuss sang opera and had a southern colonel as her fiancé; Fletcher Rabbit's problem was that his ears wouldn't stand up straight. Other peculiar charmers were in the group, all sharing freewheeling, extemporaneous times with Fran Allison. They sang, laughed, put on plays, exchanged confidences and worked out problems together. Each character was instantly recognized by its costume: the traditional stringy-haired witch in her long black dress; the bosomy,

107

ostentatiously dressed opera singer; the droopy-eared rabbit. The large Kuklapolitan clan each had its own idiosyncrasies.

Sesame Street

Jim Henson's "Sesame Street" also combined humans with puppet animals. Children have a special love and trust for animals, and animal puppets endowed with human foibles makes them especially believable. Big Bird, Miss Piggy, Kermit the Frog and the rest of the Muppets, while earning trust and celebrity, became convincing educators. Jim Henson was an extraordinary innovator. He revolutionized methods of education and his puppets are unique teachers who capture the attention of their students, unsuspectingly learning through laughter and delight.

It is only in puppetry that innovation runs its full course, for there are no inhibitions of creator or actor to stand in the way. The puppet master may devise the most outlandish costume and turn it into any creature his inventiveness will allow. He has the latitude to introduce fantasy that cannot be reproduced with live actors, for his puppets have an agility with which humans are not endowed, and upon whose bodies costumes could not function as they do on the frame of a puppet.

In his theatre on Barrow Street in New York City, Bil Baird's imagination led him in every direction, demonstrating that a wide range of ingenuity finds fertile ground in puppetry. His puppets traveled the world, and participated in every form of entertainment.

It would be a mistake to regard puppets only in the terms of entertainment or education for children. We must not forget the other branch of the puppet family: the serious and artistic puppets.

Oriental Puppetry

In the Orient the past is preserved in puppetry. Elaborately costumed figures behind a transparent screen are lighted to produce them as shadow puppets. They perform classical plays of heroic proportion encompassing philosophical, political and religious expression. Dressed in exquisite brocades and silk, delicate porcelain hand puppets of China reincarnate the figures of ancient legends.

Bunraku

Japan's Bunraku is the puppet theatre guardian of Japanese theatrical tradition and runs parallel in the classicism to the Kabuki theatre. Its ritual, learned through precise training, is unique in presentation. Each puppet appears on stage with three manipulators who guide their movements before the audience: one for each arm, another for the legs. A narrator recounts the story while accompanied by a musician.

The costumes for the puppets are carefully conceived, color and fabric scrupulously determined in accordance with the station of the life portrayed. For nobility there are the luxurious satins and embroideries in dignified hues; the colors of the courtesans' silks must be beguiling. Farmers, merchants, each is presented in traditionally correct attire, even as to fabric texture. All costumes must precisely define the character.

Costume is at the heart of Bunraku; all participants have specific traditional garments. Since the manipulators are on stage, it is necessary to eclipse their presence. The chief manipulator, who operates the puppet's right hand, wears tall clogs so that he is placed above his two assistants. He is garbed in a ceremonial black samurai kimono and wing-shouldered vest; his assistants wear hooded black robes, their faces completely obscured by hoods, and hands hidden in black thumbless gloves. Narrator and musician are identically dressed in white kimonos and blue-winged vests.

Rod Puppets

The puppets of Moscow's Central State Puppet Theatre, whose figures are supported by rods and operated beneath the stage, perform theatre so diversified that if it were comprised of live actors the repertory could not be easily duplicated. Stories and fairy tales are presented for children. Artists who have been trained within the theatre produce serious and satirical plays and entertainments, at times incorporating live actors. Their ingenuity is encouraged and reproduced in skillful and ingenious costuming.

Marionettes

Salzberg Marionette Theatre in Austria perhaps possesses the most prolific of puppets. These marionettes perform opera, ballet, and plays progressing from fairy tales to Shakespeare. Backed up by singers and musicians, they are so exquisitely costumed and expertly manipulated, that it requires no imagination to accept them as living performers.

Puppets in Opera

From the 1940s through the 1960s a puppet opera house resided within The Kungsholm, a Danish restaurant in the city of Chicago. Housed in a building of stately design, its several dining rooms provided the ambience of an intimate palace. After dinner, guests were invited to attend a performance in the opera house. It was a small, elegant theatre, the proscenium scaled to the size of its rod puppets. Recorded famous voices transported miniature opera singers to heights of grand operatic emotion. These magnificently adorned opera stars took their bows and graciously received bouquets. As the houselights went up, the entire stage suddenly filled with the round, smiling face of the puppeteer. It was the startling countenance of a giant. The audience was not yet prepared for reality.

Puppet theatre's opportunities for inventiveness are without limitation for the actor who chooses the mask of the puppet's costume. It is as much at home in every society and civilization as is theatre with live actors, with the same opportunity to offer realistic, comic, poetic or fantastic styles of presentation.

Costume is the incentive and the instrument. The eyes of detached puppet heads stare blankly into space; attached to their costumes, they sparkle with life, and are the puppeteer's inspiration. He creates their multifarious transfigurations.

Puppetry is enchanting, inventive and mysterious. The puppeteer inhabits the puppet; the puppet is part of the puppet master. Each breathes life into the other.

It is imagination. It is creativity. It is costume.

Chapter 12
FASHIONING FANTASY

"We are such stuff
As dreams are made of, and our life
Is rounded with a sleeper."
Prospero, in "The Tempest"

Theatre holds up a mirror and reflects the history of humankind, its foolishness and its fragility. To complete the portrayal of each facet of mortals, the performer endeavors to capture their fleeting fantasies and elusive dreams.

Impromptu mixtures of reality, illusion and illogical meanderings of the mind must be held fast by a fixative in order to carry them into the theatre. The fixative is costume. Since fantasies and dreams are completely free and boundless, adaptations into visible shapes are echoes of their fluidity of imagination. Unfettered by regulation, the costume and the performer become whatever inspiration invents.

Many of our classical theatrical fantasies are traceable to the medieval period, a time of probing and questioning the mysteries of man's place in the universe. Stirred by interpretations of nature's cycles, learned men contemplated movements of stars, delved into magic, attempted to decipher the Bible's enigmatic messages. Fired by fallacious assumptions, their conclusions fomented delusions and fantasies.

Costumes in Shakespearean Plays

William Shakespeare dramatized fantasies conjured by the mysterious, inexplicable elements of nature and combined them with the superstitions of his sixteenth-century contemporaries. He fashioned for the theatre the "airy nothing" of fairies, elves, spirits, ghosts and monsters, their costumes influenced by fanciful perceptions of the natural world.

Titania, the gossamer-winged, white-robed fairy queen of *A Midsummer Night's Dream* personifies vaporous drifting clouds, and elfin-green Puck the shape of a leaf set dancing by soft breezes. Monstrous Caliban of *The Tempest* resembles a twisted ancient tree, while Ariel's sparkling appearance suggests glittering star-light. Fear-provoking black, starless nights blend with the eerie shapes of the three sinister witches of *Macbeth*, and the grey ghost of Hamlet's father is as haunting as floating fogs of midnight.

Materializing Disembodied Spirits, Elves, Fairies and Witches

Actors materializing disembodied spirits are set free to be as unrestricted in movement as the nebulous contours of nature that fashion their garments of fantasy.

The manifestation of elves, fairies and witches inspired the fairy tales of the Grimm brothers. The embodiment of good and evil enkindled invention of novel and peculiar creatures of imagi-nation, and stimulated performers to mold them into recognizable and enchanting forms.

Classical tales of the fantastic have been translated by every branch of the performing arts, and they remain consistently in-triguing and fresh since unreality, free from restriction or rule, is the inspiration for inventiveness of concepts and costumes. This fertile territory is a catalyst for unique interpretations.

The performer's only clue to the nature of the fantasy figure is the costume. Phantoms and fairies do not move in the manner of humans, for they are not human. Without costume, the actor can-not begin to define the character he is representing nor its bearing and gesture, and must rely upon its garb to propel his actions.

Costume Design Follows Function

The costume is determined by the manner in which the tale is to be told. Spirits and fairies transformed into ballet figures are costumed to accentuate the willowy movement of dancers. Capable of leaping into space, the floating costume of the balle-rina's fairy queen of *A Midsummer Night's Dream* exudes an aura of magic as she becomes a fairy in flight. Since fairies aren't all alike and an actress is fastened to the ground, an earthbound Titania deftly flutters her wings and moves nimbly in her delicate raiment to accentuate the airy quality of her being.

Nijinsky's ballet, *Spectre de la Rose*, is a young girl's dream in-spired by the fragrance of the flower tenderly nestled in her hand. The rose-petaled costume enveloping the dancer invites a romantic depiction of a phantom rose entwined with the lovely dreamer.

Cinderella is the tale of a maiden's dream come true. It has been brought to life in plays, musical comedy, ballet and opera, each with its own version. Despite continual retelling of the familiar story, it is distinctive in each of the art forms. A bewitchingly lovely fairy godmother, a raggedy maiden endowed with a beguiling gown and glass slippers, and a handsome, elegant prince foster departures in costume and expression. Wicked stepmothers and their ugly daughters are presented with tempting opportunities to convert costume into comedy.

Traditionally evil figures populating the world of illusion are not limited to wicked stepmothers and witches. Beware of the devil. Christopher Marlowe produced for the stage and fixed forever the sixteenth century's image of the devil. Intrigued by the life of Dr. Faustus, a physician who experimented with magical arts, Marlowe was impressed by a Swiss pastor's declaration that Dr. Faustus was strangled by the devil. The playwright assembled these factual elements into his *The Tragical History of Doctor Faustus*, and incarnated the devil Mephistopheles, whose garments are reminders of the fires and murky shadows of hell. Faust's surrender to the devil's preferred temptations induced Goethe's poetic version, and led to an operatic adaptation of Faust's disasterous association with Mephistopheles.

The devil adopts many a guise and is at home everywhere. In theatre he has been known to make his appearance as a charming fellow who suddenly spreads wide his romantic cape to startlingly reveal that he is a fiendish vampire. At night he may become a werewolf. He has been known to shrink to the size of a puppet for the sole purpose of becoming Punch's devilish adversary. In film he has disguised himself as the neighbor next door, and is soon the calamity of the community. He frequents the opera house quite often, and not always in his familiar role as the suave and persuasive Mephistopheles, slender in tights and cape, swirling about with his customary panache. He assumes many aspects in *The Tales of Hoffman*: a wizened inventor of magical spectacles, a sly magician who steals shadows and reflections, a frock-coated doctor who coaxes a maiden to death.

Costumes Enhance Characterization

Although the devil may turn up anywhere, we are able to

detect him almost immediately, for his clothing gives him away. Even if he does not make an open declaration in red tights, curling tail and pitchfork in hand, a slight hint always exists. A red handkerchief, tucked into the breast pocket of his dark suit, adds a touch of flamboyant deviltry. We become wary of his intentions when we notice his pointed ears, or the subtle suggestion of horns in the shape of his hat. Costume and make-up details are a keynote to the actor's deliverance of the devil, from downright sinister to romantic seducer. Along the way the performer seeks to evolve his movements and interpretation by capitalizing on all the possibilities his costume affords.

Thanks to Hansel and Gretel's confrontation with a wicked witch, generations of children have become early patrons of opera. Her menacing black-caped robe and conical peaked hat encourages singers to be enthusiastically horrifying. But don't be misled by her well-established style; she is not unlike the devil. A witch, too, doesn't always come wrapped in the same package, shriveling us with cackling laughter.

She may be beguiling and sophisticated in her sleek black gown, bewitching us with an alluring manner, but arousing our suspicions when we catch glimpses of her red-lined skirt. The evil witch who screeches and violently throws her arms about might on occasion take the guise of a subtle, conniving enchantress, her actions contoured and controlled by her clothing.

The Musical "Cats"

Witches and their cats evoke sorcery, but cats, too, are many-sided. *Cats*, the musical adaptation of T. S. Eliot's poem on the subject of these haughty and mysterious creatures, provides an intriguing insight into their private lives. Their fascinating adventures could never have been realized without make-up and costume to invest the actors with the convincing appearance of cats, and induce them to freely imitate their grace and instinctive alertness.

Swan Lake Ballet

Animals have a particular charm when fantasy endows them with human qualities. They are either lovable or frightening, and the performer's artfulness with his disguise will represent the animal to be appealing or appalling. The ballet *Swan Lake* reveals that even among swans, there exists that difference.

Princess Odette and her friends turn into white swans when daylight appears, returning to human form only at nightfall. Of course, this spell was cast by an evil magician, only to be broken by a lover's eternal devotion. Prince Siegfried observes Odette's conversion from swan to maiden, and pledges his love will overcome the enchantment.

The king's throne having been vacated by his father's death, it becomes necessary for the Prince to make the immediate choice of a bride. In the guise of an ambassador to the court, the magician presents as a nuptial candidate his daughter Odile, whom he has transformed into the likeness of the beloved swan maiden.

The ballerina performs several roles: she is a maiden by night and a swan by day; her other characterization is Odile. To identify her multiple images, she wears a simple crown when she appears as the swan; as the princess her crown is jewelled. To present herself as Odile, her costume is of another color, and her make-up and hair style are altered. In each instance the ballerina's posture, attitude and movement are fashioned by her costume.

The story and beauty of enchanted swans in their lakeside domain can only be achieved by costume impressions. Although *Swan Lake* is frequently performed, varied presentations sustain its captivating quality. Only the ballet's story and Tchaikovsky's music are irrevocable. All else is open to alteration.

Ballet must rely solely upon movement to convey a story with clarity. Dancers' classic ballet steps alone will not suffice; it can only be explicitly illustrated by the performers' attire. Costume and choreography function in tandem as the framework for the dancer's inspired interpretation.

The Ring of the Nibelungs

Combining emotionally stirring music with lush costuming, opera reaches dramatic heights in fantasy. Dark legends of Richard Wagner's *The Ring of the Nibelungs* overflow with ephemeral Rhinemaidens, hairy dwarfs, and Valkyries in battle array.

Siegfried, roughly garbed in colors of the forest, removes Brunhilde's helmet and opens the fastenings of her warrior's armor to discover that underneath it all, she is wearing a dress, and thus begins a passionate love affair awakened by an appealing gown.

The Magic Flute

Wolfgang Amadeus Mozart's *The Magic Flute* has all the allure of illusion: a Queen of the Night startlingly splendid in glittering black crown and robes, a magician with power to assume any shape at will, a solemn assembly of high priests. To lighten the fantasy, birdman Papageno, covered almost completely in feathers, a large birdcage upon his back, fortified by his clown-like merry impudence, embarks upon a series of adventures. In search of a sweetheart to call his own, his only encounter is with a little old lady. But joyful fulfillment comes to Papageno when she turns into his female counterpart, a feathered and perky little Papagena.

Without the thrilling splendor of its panoply, opera's perfect blend of theatre and music would be bereft of fully realized emotional drama and appear to be a static concert recital. As in ballet, singers' performances are endowed with the benefit of wider expression when they integrate their costumes with action and music, the familiar becoming renewed by a fresh approach.

The Golem

Among the legends of the past is one that produced the prototype terrifying figure of fantasy: an inanimate object which is fashioned and brought to life by its creator who controls its actions, only to be overpowered by his own creation. The sixteenth century's fascination with mystic interpretations of religious literature produced the myth of the Golem.

The fable unfolds with the revelation that the method of constructing a Golem is to be found in sacred writings. Interpreting this mystical formula, a rabbinical scholar fashions clay into the shape of a man, and imbues it with life by placing a magical amulet upon its chest. The Golem becomes his creator's robot and servant, abides by his bidding and performs domestic tasks. In times of injustice, the Golem is a protective force. Ultimately the creature frees himself of human control, wreaks destruction and abducts his master's daughter. In a wave of compassion, he does her no harm, and eventually becomes once again a piece of lifeless clay.

The Museum of Modern Art Film Stills Archive 1 W. 53rd. Street. New York City

The Golem was introduced in an early silent movie.

The Golem was introduced in an early silent movie, the actor's costume imparting the appearance of a large, clumsy, not-quite-human figure of stone. Confined in this clumsiness, the actor moved with awkwardness and mechanized gestures, and made his debut as film's first programmed robot.

From this legend, Mary Shelley fabricated Frankenstein's monster. The only difference between the two creatures, she explained, was that her monster was a scientific creation rather than a religious one. Frankenstein's brainchild later made his screen appearance, to become the model for all the movie monsters to come.

Monsters and Robots

Monsters and robots permeate our landscape of fantasy. They remain the source of innumerable innovative transformations of inanimate objects coming to life. They, as do all citizens of the world of imagination, come in variations of the same theme. They can be decidedly beastly and menacing, or harbor a soft-hearted side. Refashioned into ingenious shapes by artists in all the performing arts, monsters inhabit prehistoric fantasies, invade the normalcy of everyday life, and are habitually inclined

119

to fall in love with beautiful women. Monsters and robots reside in science fiction's distant planets. Humans and monsters develop close bonds; robots become loyal servants to humans, or may suddenly switch gears and run amuck.

A monster or robot, despite its perceptible human characteristics, is not human, and therefore moves and performs in an uncivilized manner. There is only one way for an actor to authentically emulate its peculiarities, and that is with costume and make-up. He will then acquire, in addition to its appearance, the inducement to conduct himself in the manner befitting a monster's weirdness.

The actor's disguise delineates his performance. Figments of fantasy, embodied by costume alone, enkindle vivid dramatization and provide actors with an uninhibited sense of freedom, allowing imagination to have full reign.

Since you cannot visualize yourself as anything but human and therefore feel no other way, you need an acquaintanceship with yourself dressed as a fantasy figure. Before a mirror, study your appearance in costume. Your reflection will introduce you to the otherworldly creature you have become, and will serve as your improvisational impetus. Once familiar with your new entity, live with it as much as possible. Your costume is now you; while you are wearing it, you are bound to become what you appear to be, and your actions will reflexively develop with your newly found image.

Peter Pan

Dreams are a major element in children's tales of make-believe. Wendy dreamed of Peter Pan, the little boy who never grew up. Peter, a sprightly figure in his tights and cap with its jaunty feather, declares: "If you believe in fairies, clap your hands." It's a rare person in the audience who doesn't enthusiastically applaud. That response reveals the secret of a performer's success in achieving the illusion of fantasy: believe in what you represent and what you are wearing. Your conviction will yield a spontaneous, convincing performance.

The Wizard of Oz

Dorothy's imagination twisted reality into a dream. During her journey to the Land of Oz, she was accompanied by three workers on the family farm, a nasty neighbor and a kindly for-tuneteller. Dorothy's dream recasts the three men into a scare-crow, a tin man deprived of a heart, and a lion without courage. The neighbor became a witch, the fortuneteller turned into a wizard.

The movie version of *The Wizard of Oz* sets a standard of measure for any performer of whimsy. Ray Bolger's stuffed-with-straw scarecrow is limp, soft, bendable, and prone to falling. Jack Haley's tin man walks with stiff awkwardness, rendered motion-less when he rusts, and we suffer with him until he is rescued by the oil can. Bert Lahr, the cowardly lion, is every inch a faint-hearted beast as he nervously wrings, twists and gnaws at his tail. Along with Judy Garland's Dorothy, we accept them as real. The actors are persuaded by their costumes and conceive their performances around them.

When Dorothy awakens from her dream, her three friends are beside her, but now they are in their usual overalls. No scare-crow, no tin man, no lion. The dream and its charming characters have disappeared. The magic has vanished.

Alice in Wonderland

Long before the term "surrealistic" became a descriptive term for dreams, Lewis Carroll's *Alice in Wonderland* sketched the disjointed, illogical quality of dreams that distorts reality into alternating frustrations and delights.

Alice's adventures have been related in theatre and film, and the strange characters she meets are usually in the mold cast by the illustrations of John Tenniel. In film she has met them in a variety of configurations. The White Rabbit, The Cheshire Cat, the Mad Hatter, the King and Queen of Hearts, and all the other bizarre folk of Wonderland, have been portrayed by actors in representative costumes. Alice has also become an animated figure meeting similarly cartooned characters. A live Alice has encountered them as members of the puppet family. Actors have given voice to puppets and animated figures, conforming their speech to the actions and appearance of the costumed images.

Alice regularly appears in the theatre, and at times her odd friends are a combination of puppets and actors wearing masks, costumed as playing cards or animals. The actress portraying

Alice, invariably dressed in blue, her familiar "Alice band" holding long blonde hair in place, responds to these varied concoctions of curious creatures as if they were actual beings, their appearance instigating and influencing her reactions. The actors' applied ingenuity and particular facility of imagination will turn the entire entourage of Lewis Carroll's crackpots into credible characters of a ludicrous dream.

The Fantasy of Dreams

Nebulous configurations of waking thoughts and images linger in our minds to inhabit our dreams. Fantasies invade our waking. Everyone lives within the two worlds of waking and sleeping, seeking to bring meaning and linkage between them.

Joseph of the Old Testament, noted for his coat of many colors, stood before the ruler of Egypt and interpreted the Pharaoh's dreams. His forecasts of the future saved Egypt from starvation and reshaped the history of his people. Scrooge spent Christmas Eve in his nightrobe and cap, dreaming of his past, present, and nightmare future. Dreams altered his ways, and his prospects became a happy reality in Charles Dickens' *A Christmas Carol*. Sigmund Freud designated dreams as symbols of guilt, repression and frustration. He became the progenitor of surrealism.

He also was part of changing times. Old values and moral attitudes were rejected by the young, the First World War setting them free to follow their own inclinations. Freud spoke aloud of dreams permeated with desires and thoughts never before publicly articulated. The young shocked their elders by giving form to grotesque and fragmented dreams and called it surrealism.

Theatrical Surrealism

Surrealism penetrated the entire range of our artistic world. Sculptors, painters, musicians and dancers discovered surrealism as a fresh path to innovation. Its improvisational nature connected it to theatre. The new art of motion pictures became an ideal medium for its expression.

Extemporaneous and haphazard, it was alien to all that constituted conventional theatre where individual actors presented realistic situations to a receptive and understanding audience.

122

As in dreams, surrealistic theatre has no story line, no defined figures, and requires the audience to interpret to its own satisfaction what appears on the stage. Surrealism is the dark, jagged underside of fantasy, a mixture of Freudian nightmares, madness, cruelties, sexual exaggerations and perversities — a demoniacal demonstration of the lack of reasonableness in existence. It is unreal, illogical and nebulous as dreams. It attempts to visualize and animate the transitory which is without meaning.

This places a unique burden upon both actor and audience. So bizarre were some early theatrical surrealistic productions, on occasion puppets were employed for effects that could not have been possible for live actors to execute. The actor is treated as a puppet, losing his own individuality and becoming part of motion and action of no easily discernable significance. The costume he wears is not representative of any one person since he is a nonperson. The actor is a backdrop, part of the scenery of the undefinable emptiness of existence.

What is an actor to do? How can he manage a costume that might be a box-like placard with a word or statement lettered upon it? What if his face is made up with an eye painted upon his chin and hair flowing from his eyes, a leg disguised as an arm, and an arm that is encased in an army boot? With what can he identify himself to know how to perform in such a concoction of costume?

The actor must accept the fact that he is enacting someone else's peculiar dreamworld. Surrealism is the destruction of classical beauty, and all the grace of gesture and reality of movement that is normally required is eradicated. Just as he abandons himself to the character portrayed in traditional theatre when he assumes appropriate clothing, manners and attitudes, so must he yield to the unconventional with the identical approach, and accept unreality for the real thing.

On closer inspection, the actor will find that he is not that far removed from the mime or clown. Many of his actions may be in pantomime, or he may be expected to make outlandish gestures and be called upon to use his costume for eccentric effects, such as wearing huge balloon breasts, manipulating and then bursting them. The very distortion of costume is an encouragement to his resourcefulness and action. Both mime and clown recognize that to understand and appreciate the performance, the audience must also incorporate its own imagination. Since the actor in surrealistic theatre is not appearing in a customary manner, the unorthodox costume and mask are fundamental to his effectiveness. Nothing in the costume is realistically human, and in its own queer way grants the actor a new and stimulating leeway.

The basics of handling the costume still apply. Its very strangeness is an invitation to learn to live in it as if it is truly a part of you, for then it provokes your imagination. If the costume is awkward to wear and wield, its difficulties will make it necessary for you to make the mandatory adjustments beforehand. Fixing the actions of clown and mime firmly within your mind, treat it as a costume with a gimmick, and learn the strategy of dealing with it. Whatever your viewpoint may be of surrealism in the theatre, for an actor it's always an adventure to try something unusual. It expands the imagination and encourages inventiveness, and those assets can be beneficially transferred back to reality.

Surrealism in Movies

A torrent of illusion in motion pictures poured forth. The first outburst surfaced with *The Cabinet of Dr. Caligari*, a black and white film produced in Germany following the First World War. Its opening scene is serene. Seated upon a garden bench, a neatly and conservatively dressed young man with an air of total sobriety, is relating a story to a young gentleman sharing the bench. We then watch his tale unfold.

The surrealistic background of the opening scene reveals houses distorted by slanted angular lines. All appears to be askew. Dr. Caligari is conducting a sideshow at the city fairgrounds. His black-caped coat is worn and shabby; a top hat rests upon a head of long, straggly grey hair; round, black-rimmed eyeglasses cover eyes that gleam with connivance and malevolence. Back bent, he walks with a cane. He exhibits onstage the temporary reawakening of a man who has been locked in sleep for twenty-five years.

Attending the performance is our narrator, accompanied by his close friend and friendly rival for the affections of a young woman. The sleeper, his tall, slender form encased in closely fitting jersey top and tights, awakens to entertain the audience with

124

prophecies. His first prediction is the death of the storyteller's friend. It will occur at dawn.

The following morning the friend is found murdered. Additional murders occur in rapid succession. Soon after the young man becomes engaged to the once jointly admired girl. Cozily asleep in her bed, one night she is carried off in the arms of the Sonnambulist, her white gown floating loosely in the night breezes. Fortunately she escapes. Police call upon Dr. Caligari only to discover that the sleeping man resting within the cabinet is a dummy figure, and are left with no evidence to verify the identity of the culprit.

Believing Dr. Caligari to be both guilty and mad, our storyteller hastens to the nearby mental institution for help. Several white-coated doctors lead him to the head of the asylum. It is the venomous appearing Dr. Caligari. Judged to be insane, the young man is incarcerated. Impeccably dressed, his gray hair carefully combed, Dr. Caligari emerges once again, this time walking among his patients, his expression benign behind unrimmed eyeglasses.

As the young man ends his tale, he points out to his fellow inmate the young woman in a white flowing gown who passes by their garden bench in a trance-like state. She, he explains, is his fiancée.

What is real, and what is the fantasy of a deranged mind? Can we believe what we see? Costume gives us our clues; it gives us our doubts. The attire of the actor enabled him to elicit contradictory perceptions and induce an atmosphere of eerie unreality.

Surrealism opened wide the doors of ingenuity in film, and Luis Buñuel and Salvador Dali were among the first to pass through. Engrossed in Freud's dream theories, their innovative *Un Chien andalou* graphically depicted the distortions of reality in fragmented dreams and nightmares. The silent movie is only sixteen minutes in length, but Buñuel's influence upon surrealism in film is immeasurable.

Frederico Fellini's Film "8-1/2"

Filmmakers were inspired by other visions. Frederico Fellini brought his own apparitions to the screen. Taking a clue from the original surrealistic notion of converting the actor to a stand-in puppet, Fellini materialized personal fantasies and memories in his film *8-1/2.*

Marcello Mastroianni served as Fellini's alter ego. Fellini draped his own scarf around the actor, to push even further the sense of himself in Mastroianni. Throughout the film he is either wearing a black hat, or it is nearby, and he wears a nondescript black suit. Claudia, his perfect woman, tells him, "You dress like an old man." Later he dreams he is bathing, completely nude except for a large black hat upon his head.

Fellini not only saw clowns in terms of black and white, he viewed people within his own life in the same manner. Throughout the film, influenced by memories of his childhood, he cloaks in white clothing those who brought him happiness. Whoever was threatening or overbearing is enshrouded in black.

Guido, the central character of *8-1/2*, recuperating from a nervous breakdown, is seeking restoration of spirit in a spa. Moving in a dreamworld, he perceives grotesqueries in those whom he encounters. His perceptions of the bizarre are emphasized through visual exaggerations of every person within his purview.

Representative of her conservative attitude, Guido's wife is simply dressed and wears eyeglasses. His mistress teeters on heels too high, her fluffy fur-collared coat too tight, her fur hat absurd. His ideal woman is beautiful in white. He fantasizes a harem of seductively gowned women; nearby his approving, compliant wife, in housedress and scarf wrapped about her head, contentedly scrubs the floor. After he has thoroughly pursued all his memories, conflicts and fantasies, his final daydream brings together every participant in his life. All are in white.

Costume is a dominating element in Fellini's film. He uses them as symbols, distortions and impressions of character. Adapting costume for these effects, his actors take their cue and transform their individual roles into his fantasy conceptions. It also frees them to improvise their own actions in those many fleeting and transitory moments between reality, fantasies and memories.

Theatre, too, combines reality with otherworldliness. Each of playwrights Genêt, Beckett and Ionesco innovatively expressed man's loneliness and helplessness in a large, cruel and empty world, representing him not as an individual but as mankind.

Jean Genêt's Play, "The Balcony"

The actor pursues the dictates of his costume, and to establish the point of his fantasy, Jean Genêt's *The Balcony* could not have been performed without its prevalent use.

The play's action is centered in a brothel catering to the desires of a clientele to play roles in an imaginary world which is closed to them in their real existence. A gas man arrives at the brothel in his company's truck to act out his fantasy to be a pious and understanding prelate. Relishing his sense of religious authority in the magnificent robes of a bishop, in accordance with his request, a lady of the establishment portrays a confessor of abominable sins. He benevolently bestows a bishop's forgiveness upon her; his acted-out fantasy is his ecstacy.

Another patron, in the handsome uniform of an army general, is accompanied into battle by his horse, in reality a member of the brothel. Pretending to fight bravely beside his men, he finds his satisfaction in a fanciful enactment of a hero's glorious death. A third gentleman has donned judicial robes to preside over a make-believe courtroom. Correctly white-wigged, he administers justice to a confessed thief, accommodatingly portrayed by a girl of the bordello. There his dream to become a supreme court justice comes true.

All this game of pretend in the brothel takes place against the background of a country in revolution. In order to bring peace to the nation, the three men are called upon by the chief of police to put their fantasy identifications to practical use. Assuming the roles of the leaders banished by the insurrection, they ride through the city, and later appear on the balcony overlooking the city square.

The bishop blesses the crowd and forgives their insurrection; the general reviews the troops as they proudly march before him; the supreme court justice reassures them that lawfulness is restored. The crowd accepts their positions of leadership solely upon the basis of their costumed identities. The three discover that all they need to maintain their esteemed positions is to remain in their costumes. Later, the leader of the rebel force and the police chief of the loyalists, each completely stripped of clothing, find they have lost both position and identity in the revolution.

The message is apparent to the audience and the actor. You are what you wear. What you wear, you become. Clothing provides full opportunity for fabrication and realization.

Beckett's Theatre of the Absurd

Although at first glance costume would appear to be minimal in Samuel Beckett's Theatre of the Absurd, it is of subtle importance. The two tramp figures in *Waiting for Godot* are reminiscent of Charlie Chaplin's tramp; in combination, they comprise something of a vaudeville act. So essential to the essence of the play is the sense of vaudeville, Bert Lahr was cast as Gogo in the play's initial Broadway production. Lahr, who brought his superb skill as a pantomimist to burlesque and musical comedy, captured the elements of the play. To understand the nature of the characters Gogo and Didi is to recall the clown: hopeless, hapless, expectant.

While they were waiting around for Godot, others decided to actively seek answers to questions involving the extraterrestrial. Apparently extraterrestrial folk were equally curious about our planet. The first alien sojourn to Earth was undertaken by Superman, making his initial appearance in comic strips, followed by a television series. Genuine star material, he was the lead in a Broadway musical, and afterward it was on to Hollywood. There Superman found the perfect vehicle for his round-trip journeys from his adopted planet to outer space: the motion picture screen.

Costume and Superman

Costume enabled Superman to perform tasks he could not do in his everyday Clark Kent business suit. His flights into space necessitated a change into more suitable clothing, and his belief in the power of his own version of a space suit facilitated his soaring into the great beyond. Both actor and viewers are persuaded that clothing is the basis of his ability, and his flights of fantasy are plausible accomplishments.

Illusions in Television and Films

The television and movie screen is an ideal conveyance of illusion; the medium allows for special effects to make imaginative journeys to unknown territories possible and credible. Adventures of science fiction cannot be depicted without the actor's total immersion into his costume and the devices conceived to make him an explorer of those realms of imagination.

Approaches to costume remain the same as in other areas of fantasy, since there is a crossover between classical and contemporary conceptions. The ingredients of good and evil remain, continuing to be delineated by white and black. Outer space, as is currently conceived, is populated by an updated version of robots, and monsters made hideous by costumes and masks.

H. G. Wells' "Things to Come"

The film version H. G. Wells' *Things to Come* presented first glimpses and predictions of the future. Wars devastate the planet, peoples' clothing is reduced to ragged coverings. Their chieftain wears a shaggy fur vest to set him apart and serve as a symbol of his rough justice. A man of intellect and science appears to rebuild and restore Earth, a heroic figure in tights, tunic and imposing rectangular helmet. He strides with authoritative competence, imparting the promise of hope for a peaceful, technologically advanced society. The actor, Raymond Massey, disclosed all these impressions with his commanding use of costume. As the renewed civilization moves forward, clothing changes with the times: tunic and tights for men, women in short skirts and broad-shouldered bodices.

Reminiscent of the devil, villains with pointed beards make their entrance in long black robes for the purpose of impeding progress. Although there are objections to moon exploration, the leader of the proposed expedition, heroic in a white, broad-shouldered tunic, tights and cape, vows his dedication to the proposed mission.

Things to Come was an amazingly accurate forecast of the world's future, and the costumes of the subsequent science fiction movies.

"Forbidden Planet" Motion Picture

Film took men and their space suits into the outer reaches. One of the earliest journeys was to the *Forbidden Planet*, inhabited by a robot and two humans: a father and daughter. Dressed in what was then referred to as futuristic costuming, notable for its wide shoulders, the girl in tunic and miniskirt, the man in a dark jumpsuit. Walter Pidgeon and Anne Francis have a co-star, Robby

129

the Robot, among the first of his kind in outer space, and they welcome this inanimate object as a fellow performer. Imagination and improvisation, spurred on by costume and special effects, found a new home on strange planets.

Interplanetary Creatures

It was inevitable that Earth's opportunity would arrive for a visit from interplanetary neighbors, and so it came to pass with *Invasion of the Body Snatchers* and *I Married a Monster From Outer Space*. These aliens are devoted to inhabiting the bodies of unsuspecting humans. In their natural state they are revealed as full-fledged monsters with huge heads, hideous faces and elongated fingers, bodies encased in tunic and tights. Make-up and imagination produce the opportunity for actors to give vent to a convincingly frightening performance.

Special effects brought *Close Encounters of the Third Kind* and a more congenial alien to earth in the shape of one elongated white figure with huge, compassionate eyes. Appealing *E.T.* established more intimate friendships on Earth. Special effects are not unrelated to surrealism, an actor accepting them on the same basis: what is not actual is treated as reality. His response to these special effects must be creative and convincing.

Planet of the Apes

Earth and outer space are joined in *Planet of the Apes*, a motion picture fantasy that could not have been persuasively performed without costume and make-up. The wonders of make-up artists' present-day techniques of constructing and molding shapes of extraordinary likenesses of animals, horrific or realistic heads and faces, far remove the actor from the primitive masks once held over the face to simulate characters. The familiar faces of Maurice Evans, Roddy McDowall, Kim Hunter and James Whitmore were completely obliterated by costume and make-up. Inspired and motivated by their unusual but authentic appearance, each actor gestured and moved with accuracy of characterization.

The adventures on television, and later on the motion picture screen, of "Star Trek" and Mr. Spock with the pointed ears, fully familiarized actors and audience with outer space and the inhabitants of newly found planets. *Star Wars* pressed onward, introduc-

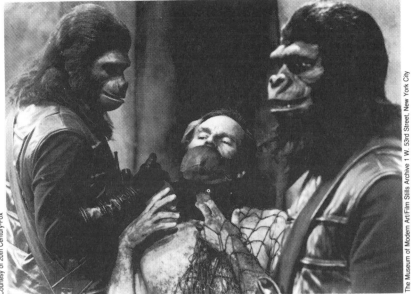

Courtesy of 20th Century-Fox

The Museum of Modern Art/Film Stills Archive 1 W. 53rd Street, New York City

"Planet of the Apes"

ing occupants of another planet, a combination of humans, robots and human shapes transformed by grotesque heads. The classic elements nevertheless endure in *Star Wars*. The princess to be rescued is white-robed; the Power of Force is in a monk's robe; black and white remain the representation of evil and goodness; the robots harbor human elements; monsters are threatening and mysterious.

On the movie and television screens, outer space has become accustomed territory, a modern version of the Old West and its cowboys and Indians, with costumes as standardized. Because the costume of adventurers in space has become almost conventional, the actor may find himself intimately familiar and comfortable with it. He is provided with the immediate characterization of an explorer of outer space, as instantaneous an identity as if he were clothed as a cowboy or Indian. Imagination is then effortlessly stirred to accept the illusion.

Fanciful Special Effects

Special effects require a particularly fanciful approach. Fay Wray was among the first of performers called upon to act as if a constructed figure were a live entity. *King Kong* became a fan-

131

tasy star, but Fay Wray verified the illusion. As the witch in *The Wizard of Oz*, Margaret Hamilton flew on a broomstick. Christopher Reeve breezed through space as Superman. All were special effects with which the actors became acquainted as an aid to the creation of illusion.

Fantasy is an exercise of the mind without restriction, and its interpretation and realization is equally without limitation of inventiveness. Dreams and fantasies add special charm to musical comedy. Laurie of *Oklahoma!* dreams of provocative girls luring cowboys riding imaginary horses. Liza in Kurt Weill's *Lady in the Dark*, influenced by her psychiatrist's analysis, casts friends and lover as circus performers in her spectacular dream. *Finian's Rainbow*, Burton Lane's musical, produced a lovable leprochaun, and *The Phantom of the Opera* combined special effects and costume to create an elaborate world of aversion and beauty.

Stories comprised of imagery are endlessly retold and recast. The inventiveness and development of infinite re-creations and combinations of methods of depiction depends upon the proficiency of performers to utilize their costumes, which is the only means by which fantasy has form. Costumed apparitions in film and theatre have provided guardian angels from heaven, with or without wings, friendly or hostile ghosts visiting earthly mortals, and glimpses of heaven with St. Peter waiting at the gates. Visions born of imagination are embellished by their improvisational nature, allowing the same tale to appear as a new adventure, retaining all of its freshness.

Just as surrealism became a turning point in imaginative use of costume through the establishment of innovative ideas, another explosion of theatrical fantasies was fostered by new technologies and the advancement of exploration into outer space. Unique art forms assimilate the products of a forward-looking age. They include constantly varying types of fabrics, laser beams, adaptations by computer. Currently there are many studios developing original techniques in the molding of special effects, masks, headgear and hair pieces, offering novel approaches to actors' presentations.

Yet unimagined vistas await the purveyors of fantasy. Tomorrow will bring an enlarged choice of yet undeveloped properties and fresh concepts of an approaching era. Inventiveness in art relies upon the talent and ingenuity of the performer to advance into the area of continual discoveries, and to make them part of costume and performance.

Imagination weaves illusion, costume enhances illusion. Abandoning himself to them, the actor symbolizes beauty, adventure, mystery and delight, those inviting domains to which we temporarily escape.

Fantasy is imagination, innovation and improvisation. Fantasy is costume.

Chapter 13
ACTING WITHOUT TRADITIONAL COSTUMES OR SCENERY

Since theatre, as in all arts, is an arena for creativity, there is always a desire for innovation. In the course of innovation there have been times when stages have been without scenery and actors without costumes. While this is a natural occurrence during rehearsal, it is quite another situation to present a theatrical performance without these usual aids. Just how successful has this proven to be?

To start with the bare basics, one of the most popular theatrical productions has been *Oh! Calcutta!*, its success focusing on the novelty of all the actors appearing in the nude — a complete revelation in its time. It was a kind of stunt with a message, but it forged no permanent path where others were compelled to follow. What it did do was introduce nudity into serious theatre. There are occasions when actors appear on stage without clothing because the situation in the play ostensibly warrants it.

Some have said that complete nudity in present-day theatre reflects the permissiveness and openness of this era; others state that if it is part of the action of the play it is acceptable. Too often nudity is introduced for sheer shock value when it isn't needed; the identical scene could be acted out, perhaps to greater advantage, with just a suggestion of nudity, or none at all.

In *Equus*, when the young girl removed her clothing and writhed among the horses, the flow of the play seemed to have halted because of the audience's reaction to the moment of titillation. It is a moot point as to whether it enhanced the performance since the audience, already aware of what was afoot through advance publicity, seemed to be alerted for "the moment."

Nudity Is a Distraction for Actors and Audiences

Only among those few fortunately blessed is the human figure perfectly endowed and for most actors it takes a certain degree of courage to appear on-stage more than barefaced before an audience. Since clothing functions as a disguise for the actor, completely revealing himself in the nude not only creates a self-consciousness, with no place to hide, but makes it more difficult for him to forget self and be immersed in his role. The audience, too, shares this consciousness of nudity and is inclined to be distracted by it, thus destroying the element of immersion necessary for both the actor and the spectator.

The suggestion of nudity, rather than complete nudity, is in its own way more provocative and tantalizing, emphasizing the attitude of the character rather than creating the inevitable distraction of complete nudity. Constant nudity also has a tendency to lose its shock value and does an about-face by becoming boring. Florenz Ziegfeld's famous *Follies* demonstrated the allure of the veiled nude. He realized that this form of costuming was more exciting to an audience than a completely bare body, which can sometimes be offensive, whereas the veiled nude presents a form of artistic beauty.

On-stage boudoir scenes have been done by fully clothed actors, leaving much to the imagination of the audience. Christopher Hampton's adaptation of Pierre Laclos' *Les Liaisons Dangereuses* contained a lusty bedroom encounter made all the more evocative because both man and maid were dressed. If it had been performed by nude actors, it could well have spoiled the quality of the seduction scene and destroyed the playwright's original intention.

Bare Stage Productions

Many times producers have experimented by presenting classical plays without costume or set — just the bare stage. As a novelty for both the actor and the audience it was considered most ingenious, for it was thought to be a welcome departure from the usual. At times this innovative approach has met with a degree of success. However, it presents a tremendous challenge for the actors to perform well and believably.

Innovational and Improvisational Costuming

Shakespearean plays in particular have served as a basis for a great deal of costume innovation. In order to underscore the universality of William Shakespeare's plays, they have been presented in costumes indicative of time periods and places other than originally situated, ranging through succeeding centuries up to our time, with backgrounds from First Empire France to modern Mexico. In many productions "the time has been out of joint."

Sir John Gielgud was directing Richard Burton in *Hamlet*, and he strived to do something unusual since he felt he otherwise would be presenting a carbon copy of years of past productions. Because Burton did not feel comfortable in Elizabethan clothing and Gielgud was impelled toward the innovative, he proposed to stage the play as if it were a rehearsal, with the actors in modern dress, using improvised props. It was determined that a walking stick or an umbrella would serve as a sword, and it would be acceptable to have an overcoat represent a cape. Each actor was responsible for the selection of his own costume, and while everyone spent liberal amounts of money, nothing seemed to be right. The King selected a variety of hats, blazers and slacks. The Queen assumed that the mink coat she chose would announce her royalty, but it didn't seem to work. Nevertheless, they went ahead and performed in their clothing selections upon a bare, bleak set. The audience, Gielgud discovered, had absolutely no idea what it was all about.

The background of Shakespeare's *Hamlet* is the splendor and regality of the court and that bare stage could not effectively depict it nor give the actors that feeling of royalty an appropriate set could have accomplished. The modern clothes could not impart the sense of royalty which would have inspired both Hamlet and the mink-coated actress had she been gowned in Queen Mother Gertrude's dark velvets. An Ophelia enveloped in the ethereal quality of a chiffon robe delicately evokes for her and Hamlet the touching pathos of their situation. Each actor is not only influenced by his own costume, but the costumes of those with whom he is performing. Appropriate costuming can and does inspire an actor to give a better performance.

The joy of Shakespeare lies in the text, and if the costuming does not match the text, it can result in ludicrous confusion. There are many instances in Shakespeare's plays that allude to the costume, making it pivotal to the plot. In *As You Like It* Rosalind and Celia plan to run off to the Forest of Arden and Rosalind, typical of any woman going away on a journey, discusses with Celia what she should wear:

"Were it not better
Because thát I am more than common tall
That I did suit me all points like a man?"

Dressed as a man, she is suddenly agitated when she learns that Orlando is near by, for she doesn't want him to see her thus garbed, and panics:

"Alas the day! What shall I do with my doublet
and hose?"

In our present era, with women so often dressed in clothing imitative of men, a modern-dress *As You Like It* would completely reduce Rosalind's consternation into nonsense. Many of Shakespeare's comedies and their twists and turns are a merry melee of costumes, and without them their humor and fun would sorely suffer.

Time, costume and attitude are reflected in Shakespeare's plays, and since clothing is representative of the period, his references to fashion are a natural part of his text.

While Petruchio is devoting himself to taming his shrew, he demolishes Katherine's joy in a new dress she is wearing to please him, and he denounces the current fashion with ridicule:

"What, this a sleeve? 'Tis like a demi-cannon . . ."

A modern-day Katherine in jeans and shirt would be destructive to such a scene.

Suppose, desiring to prove once again Shakespeare's good-for-all-times-and-places, a director decides to introduce novelty and places *The Merchant of Venice* in present-day Memphis, Tennessee. In one scene Portia, discussing the young Falconbridge, a baron of England, evaluates him to Nerissa:

"How oddly he is suited! I think he bought his doublet
in Italy, his round hose in France, his bonnet in
Germany, and his behavior everywhere."

Odd indeed in modern Memphis!

The practices of the time in which Shakespeare placed his
plays are referred to in the text. During the period of Hamlet's
tragic turmoil, it was considered appropriate for a man to continually have a hat on his head, whether he was in or out of doors. A
bare-headed man would be considered not to have all of his wits
about him. So Ophelia expresses to Polonius concern for Hamlet,
her suspicions of his agitation aroused by his disarrayed clothing:

"Lord Hamlet, with his doublet all unbraced,
No hat upon his head; his stockings fouled,
Ungartered, and down-gyved [hanging] to his ankle;
Pale as his shirt . . . "

How would a modern-dress Hamlet solve that one?

Laurence Olivier had an intimate knowledge of Richard III,
and considered him to be a man much devoted to his own appearance and the necessity of wearing the proper clothing for a particular situation. He noted that after Richard has met with Lady
Anne and properly charmed her, he's delighted with his own
image, and speaks of it to the sun:

"Shine out, fair sun, till I have bought a looking glass,
That I may see my shadow as I pass."

A Richard clad in an elaborate lace-trimmed costume for his
meeting with Lady Anne would indeed cast a handsome shadow.
If, however, he wore a modern business suit, what urgent need
would he have of a substitute mirror to silhouette his ordinary
appearance?

When deprived of appropriate costuming, the finest Shakespearean actor has an enormous burden since it puts him in conflict
with the text, the time, the attitude, the very essence of the plays.
Perhaps scenery can be dispensed with, but the performer is reinforced and enhanced by his costume. If it does not serve him as
intended, nor he serve the costume, the performer is hampered,
for he cannot do justice to the play and his own interpretation.

Shakespeare has nourished us well. We should do as much for him.

Traditional Costumes are Often Required

Without traditional costuming some plays would completely lose both their meaning and message. Female roles in Chinese opera are performed by men. In David Hwang's play, *M. Butterfly*, based upon factual events, a Chinese male opera singer carried his impersonation of a woman into his private life as a spy, thereby entrapping a French diplomat to China into a love affair. So lovely, appealing and graceful was the actor, who demurely refused to remove his clothing before the lover, his deception was successful. It was achieved by the actor's dependence upon magnificent kimonos to contribute to the illusion of femininity; the movement of the drapery and the fluidity of its silk kimonos gave the actor the feeling and attitude of an exquisite and beguiling female. Movement, beauty and style were the natural result of an actor's intelligent use of his costumes, and his eventual removal of his kimono, make-up and wig presented a dramatic revelation that would have been absolutely impossible to effect without them.

The necessity of expressive coordination of costume with script is the mainstay of both actor and director; its influence on the actor is manifold, for it declares the style and manner of the play. The theatre is part of our heritage; the costume is an adjunct to its definition and preservation.

PART III:
PUTTING THE COSTUME TO USE

Chapter 14
THE AUDITION

You know the part is just made for you, and are ready to answer the call-up. But are you ready? Have you prepared for the part? You may reply: "What is there left to prepare since I've been training for years? I know my craft, I am sure of my talent, and I am exactly right for the role." When you come to the audition you will be in the company of many other actors sharing the same convictions. If the play is a familiar one, you've had the opportunity to read it and have a good idea about the character. In fact, you have mastered many lines of the part, rehearsed them at home, and feel fully qualified. So does almost every actor at the audition.

Then what is going to set you apart from them and convince the casting director you are the one to be selected? You have to resort to something that will aid you in your interpretation beyond reading lines.

The Importance of Clothes You Wear to an Audition

We return to the importance of the costume to the actor in order to *become* the character, thereby setting a two-way path: one to the actor and one to the audience. Therefore it is necessary to carefully select the clothes you are going to wear for the audition, not only to establish your suitability to the part but to demonstrate your own enthusiasm for the role which you wish to obtain. How important is enthusiasm? It is the nucleus of all creative art. An actor's enthusiasm for what he is going to wear in a play foretells what he will achieve with his costume in performance.

Kim Novak

Actors often apply for a job dressed the way they believe the character may appear. Kim Novak, an unknown actress at the time of the casting of William Inge's *Picnic*, was granted an interview with the director, Joshua Logan. She was seeking the part of Millie, a tomboy, but was apprehensive because she thought Joshua Logan would consider her too mature to portray a boyish character. She asked and received permission to read in costume. Her shiny face free of make-up, she dressed in blue jeans, a man's shirt hanging over them, and she jauntily perched upon her head a small Confederate corporal's cap. Kim Novak fulfilled a prerequisite: she displayed her enthusiasm for the part. By presenting herself in this fashion, she convinced herself that she was right for it. Most important of all, she also imprinted that fact upon Joshua Logan and ultimately upon the audience. This was achieved because she instinctively knew that appropriate costuming was the key to turning a woman into the urchin sister of Madge.

Lillian Gish

Even a well-established actress faces the challenge of persuading a director she is suitable for a role and will turn to the use of convincing attire to plead her case. Such was the situation for Lillian Gish when Guthrie McClintic brought his production of *Hamlet* with John Gielgud to New York in 1936. McClintic asked Gielgud to consider whether Lillian Gish would be suitable for the role of Ophelia.

This request stirred an old memory within Gielgud. He recalled that back in the old silent film days he gazed at the advertisement of Lillian Gish and her sister Dorothy, which consisted of a photograph of the backs of a pair of small girls, both wearing straw hats. Underneath the photograph was the caption: "Two little strangers about whom all the world will soon be talking." Upon the release of D. W. Griffith's *Orphans of the Storm* introducing the appealing sisters, the prediction came true. And now, so many years later, here was Lillian Gish appearing before him in his dressing room wanting to be cast as young Ophelia.

She came to the meeting with Gielgud wearing a light summer dress with short sleeves. A large white straw hat trimmed with black velvet ribbons rested upon her fair hair. When he commented to her that the manner in which she was dressed reminded him of her photograph in the advertisement, she replied that she deliberately recreated that image in order to convince him that she was not too old to play Ophelia. Her appearance did persuade Gielgud, and she became Ophelia to his Hamlet.

Dorothy Dandridge

The necessity to prove suitability for a role is not confined to the theatre. Dorothy Dandridge was certain that she would be the ideal Carmen in the movie *Carmen Jones*. Her view was not shared by its director, Otto Preminger, who was of the opinion that she was too sophisticated.

Not discouraged, she rushed over to Max Factor's studio and unearthed an old wig which was just what she had in mind, despite the fact she was told Cornell Wilde had worn it in one of his movies. In wardrobe she tried on a bedraggled but brilliantly colored blouse, which she pulled off of one shoulder. A further search revealed a skirt that moved sensuously. Satisfied with her costume, she went to work on her wig. Standing before a mirror, she turned its ends around her face and fashioned them into spit curls, and then applied a heavy amount of lipstick. In the mirror she saw the reflection of the hussy she created. She slinked around in her bits-and-pieces costume, feeling like a thoroughgoing whore.

In her contrived costume and make-up, Dorothy Dandridge sauntered into Preminger's view the next day. He gazed at her in amazement. "My God," he exclaimed, "it's Carmen." She and her costume achieved the objective.

Since the play for which you are auditioning is a play set in the 1940s, you have decided to wear one of the more attractive dresses in your wardrobe and a pair of high-heeled shoes. However, there is a way to develop a mood that will deepen your interpretation for yourself and convince the director. "Mood" is the key word, and one of the surest ways to create a mood is through use of color. The effect of color on the actor as well as the audience is dynamic, for color paints a picture of the person portrayed.

The Importance of Color Selection

Let us suppose the role for which you hope to be chosen is that of a sophisticated woman. First of all, you will want to select a dress in which you feel comfortable and can move with ease, and know that it is becoming to you. While making your choice, bear in mind that it would be difficult, no matter how well you read your lines, to easily convince the casting director of your

145

worldliness if you are wearing a pale pink dress. Try red or black, or a combination of both colors, and he'll keep his eyes on you and believe that you are indeed sophisticated. And so will you feel that you are a worldly woman, for the colors you are wearing tell you so.

The Choice of Hair Style

For further emphasis upon your suitability, change your usual hair style, if it is casual. Before you appear for your audition, experiment with an upswept style, or part your hair in the middle, pulling it sleekly away from your face. Find the one becoming way to wear your hair that will also contribute to your feeling of sophistication.

The Use of Props

As an actor you know the word "prop." In the theatre world it is an abbreviation for "property." A prop is not physically attached to either the costume or the scenery; it is a movable accessory. Its very mobility is a useful adjunct to your acting. A handkerchief, a hat, a chair, and a tennis racket can each become an acting tool. The same word has another meaning, defined as a "support." Although that particular definition is not one generally used in the theatre, it can be applied for your own particular use, for support is exactly what you need now to help you build your belief in your ability to appear suitable for the role.

Therefore you will add a prop in the form of a pair of black gloves. Together with your new hair style, the black and red dress, that pair of black gloves used adroitly either by the motions of your gloved hands or drawing them from your hands slowly while speaking your lines, you are underscoring the image of the woman. Although you do not wear a costume, by using colors in your own dress, an appropriate hair style, and carrying a pair of gloves, you will convey to yourself, as well as the casting director, the type of person you are capable of representing.

Capturing the Spirit

For the same play that is being cast, you are an actor who is seeking the part of a recently returned veteran of World War II who has been wounded in action. Before your audition, you go to a thrift shop and find a drab-colored, ill-fitting suit that will

146

immediately give you just the reaction a soldier would experience when he comes home to find in his closet only out-of-date suits that no longer fit. With that necessary enthusiasm for the role you wish to obtain, you visit your barber and acquire a crew cut. Your appearance has now taken on that of a former soldier. Furthermore, since the script indicates that he sustained a leg injury, you assume that he limps and, when you appear onstage for your audition, you will walk across it with the use of a cane.

With the judicious choice of color, hair style, and a small, easy-to-carry, easy-to-use prop, you have each created a mood and a picture which will enhance your lines and their delivery. You have set yourselves apart from the others in your attitude and appearance.

Chapter 15
REHEARSAL AND PREPARATION

The play's the thing, but the costume helps make it so. The costume is not just icing on the cake; it is an essential ingredient. Whether working from inside out or outside in, the character's dress is an integral part of the manifestation. David Warfield defined acting at its best as a physical representation of a mental picture. Laurette Taylor embraced that definition as well, and coupled it with the projection of an emotional concept.

If yours is the "method approach" — to emotionalize the character — so be it. If it is an "Olivier approach" — to visualize the character — continue on. When one is endeavoring to create a portrait, whether it be the actor's conception or the conception of a painter, there is no reason to dispute the point as to how the representation should be developed. Whatever the choice, without your entire utilization of all the aspects of the costume, neither path will lead to a complete realization of the role.

You have learned to use your body and voice as your instrument through movement, breathing, awareness, concentration, discipline and diction. Taking all these carefully acquired attributes, the costume molds and directs them into that special character you are creating so that you, just as the Kabuki actor, once in costume and make-up sits before a mirror and focuses upon his altered image, can assume a new personality.

Before Costume Designers

As recently as the last century, costume designers did not exist in the theatre and it was up to the actor to provide his wardrobe. Otis Skinner traveled with his own furnishings of wigs and costumes. Because he and other actors during and before his time had the responsibility of the acquisition and care of their wardrobes, they were acutely aware of their dependency upon costumes in interpreting the roles for which they were famous.

Through this intimacy with them, they acquired a highly developed use and sense of theatrical clothing.

Requirements of the Actors of Today

Today's actor has need for even more intense study of the costume since he is accustomed to the casual, relaxed attire of our era. He is not bound by the discomfort of restrictive clothing; jogging shoes and low heels make for easy walking. Therefore, he has a great deal to prepare in the essential discovery and use of his costumes. Even modern dress comes in variety and, if you are primarily a jeans wearer and feel most at ease in casual clothes, you may find yourself in trouble if you are depicting a character whose usual clothing is of a more formal, dress-up mode.

We are only at home in our modern clothes. To presuppose that it is a simple matter to immediately adapt ourselves to the fashion of an age in which we have not lived is fallacy. Not to master the ability of adaptation long before dress rehearsal is a disservice to yourself and the audience. You cannot be only *part* of the time and period; you must be *all* of the time and period.

Aside from the necessary "at homeness" in the costume, how are you going to fully understand the character if you do not analyze his choice of clothing, with its color and textures, and how he uses it? By fully investigating and using every aspect of your costume you provide yourself with an important tool of acting. It will alter your posture, stance and gestures, whether it is one of an elegant gentleman or a pathetically poor man. Surely there are few individuals, and most particularly actors, who have not gazed into the mirror to find the substance behind their faces. Just as we constantly discover new facets of our own beings, a probing of the character to be enacted brings endless discoveries into the depth of his being, his clothes reflecting his nature.

Dirk Bogarde

Dirk Bogarde looks to the clothing the character would select for himself as a key to the development of the role. For the film of Harold Pinter's *The Servant*, he was grateful for the costume designers's thoroughness in every detail. He was provided with a shiny blue serge suit, a patterned nylon scarf crossed over a tight, mended sweater, a pork-pie hat embellished with a feather, and black shoes with a slight squeak. The mediocre, seedy garments indicated to him the mediocre, seedy nature of the servant. The clothing disclosed the man and served the actor's performance.

Consider a priest in his private surroundings. Relaxed and away from public eyes, he appears no different than any other man at leisure in his home. Nor does he feel any other way. But when he is to appear in public, as he steps into his robe and places the hard white collar around his neck, he has changed his appearance from that of an ordinary man into a defined, recognizable priest. His robes alter his movements, the hard collar compels him to move his head in another manner. His garments immediately state the fact that he is a representative of his religion, a man who conveys authority and compassion. His clothing obliges him to know and feel he is a priest. As the man sits, stands and walks in his garments, he proclaims to himself and others that he is a priest. He can be no one else.

Costume's Function in Transforming the Actor

The actor, just as with the priest, becomes different in demeanor upon assuming his public role. Unlike the priest, the actor before the public varies his appearance each time he undertakes a new part. He is always changing, constantly in the state of flux. That is the actor's reason for being. Many actors say they enjoy acting because it enables them to escape from themselves and become *another person.* The costume is an instantaneous and exciting transformation, and there are diverse ways in which it provokes this magic for actors, visually and emotionally.

At the very moment when a performer dons his costume, he begins to feel and become the character. A new and different wardrobe is the actor's aid to becoming a new and different person. But he must begin to absorb the effect it impels for a long period of time prior to the impact of the moment when he assumes the full costume for the first time. Although you may feel secure in your acting ability, you cannot take it for granted that once you are in costume you will immediately utilize it to fully define the character and automatically have the prowess to use it appropriately, comfortably and without awkwardness.

Appropriate dress creates an attitude and serves the actor as a stimulant. Although many years had passed, Cathleen Nesbitt

151

could still recall the impact of her gown when she appeared in Henry James' *Portrait of a Lady*. She was given the most elaborate costume, which was designed by Cecil Beaton. Playing the role of Countess Gemini, it imbued her with the necessary sense of authority.

The Actor and the Costume Designer

An actor, intent upon a fully developed characterization, will request the aid of the costume designer. More often than not, it will be pleasing to the designer to know the actor cares enough about his role to pay attention to what is being created for him and give it his full appreciation. You will also discover that there are some designers who prefer to talk over with the actor aspects of the costume, for the designer is your friend who is giving his creation, just as heartfelt as yours, over to your care. If it is not a period play, the designer may want to get to know you well enough so as to be able to judge what type of clothing is suitable for you in your particular role. There are occasions when clothing is purchased rather than designed, and the costumer, sometimes together with the actor, will search out what is proper for both the role and the performer.

Learning to Move in Costume

Now that you have seen your costume and tried it on, but it is not yet available to you until dress rehearsal, ask the designer if you may have the cape you are to wear, or a mockup, so that in privacy you will learn to handle it, feel it, act in it. As an aid to your performance, become familiar with the weight of your costume and the manner in which it drapes. If it is impractical or impossible to obtain that portion of your costume which is essential to your interpretation, we will discuss further on how you may assist yourself with improvised costuming.

If you are in a period play, nothing can prepare you better for it than to get the feeling of the clothing as soon as possible. Rehearsing with a long petticoat, breeches, ruffs and hats will accustom you in conducting yourself in such unfamiliar garb. You will also have the advantage of practicing ways of using the costume in order to achieve certain dramatic effects.

Margaret Webster, a director as well as an actress, directed José Ferrer when he played the role of Iago in *Othello*. He was coming to rehearsal in sneakers and shorts, and spoke his lines while keeping his hands in his pockets. She pointed out to him that since his costume for the production was a doublet and high boots, he was not properly preparing himself. As befits a concerned actor, he appeared in boots at the next rehearsal and used his deft hands for vivid gesturing.

Action With Costume and Lines

The use of the costume, or key parts of it, can also assist you in learning your lines, since while you are mastering the action necessitated by the costume and its accompanying accessories and props, your action will be suited to the words you are learning. It is important to start work early so that action and words become second nature. Your solo work is preparation for rehearsal, during which you must take into consideration the effect of the movement and effect of your costume together with those of the other actors. When you then come to rehearsal you will be prepared with your own business. If it does not meet with approval, you can change it. Nevertheless, this combination of action with costume and lines will have already served its purpose since your character is on the way to becoming more fully realized. Your costume is not a substitute but an aid in your characterization since physical elements are controlled by it. Transformation can only be completed by use of costume, since it determines gesture, and its color affects emotion.

Laurence Olivier

Each actor develops his own techniques in acquainting himself with the person he is to ultimately become. In his mind's eye, Laurence Olivier painted a portrait of the man as if he were creating an oil painting. With that then fixed image, he proceeded to bring to life his manner, movement, gestures and walk. This he accomplished alone, since he preferred not to take up rehearsal time with practice of those details more easily developed in solitude.

Dirk Bogarde

Dirk Bogarde's development of Gustav von Ashenbach in the filming of Thomas Mann's *Death in Venice* began with the gradual evolution of a costume. Never losing sight of the fact that the story was based upon Gustav Mahler, his first step was to visualize the type of clothing this man would have worn in his waning years.

He found a white, secondhand suit appropriate to the period of the First World War, and a flat-brimmed white hat. To complete his authentic wardrobe, he wore boots fastened by buttons. Observing himself in the mirror, he was satisfied that he appeared to be Mahler. When he presented himself to Visconti, who was directing the film, Visconti's delighted enthusiasm confirmed the initial efforts of his appearance.

Make-up provided the shape of Mahler's nose. Bogarde then discovered a full, greying moustache in a box of moustaches, and mixed in with buttons, pins and beads in still another box, he found pince-nez glasses with a long gold chain. With a long beige, woolen scarf around his neck, and a walking stick selected out of a pile, this assemblage of clothing, make-up and props completed the portrait of von Ashenbach-Mahler. The visual aspect accomplished, it became Dirk Bogarde's springboard to the age and emotions of von Ashenbach. The buttoned boots helped him to recall and imitate his grandfather's walk. His immersion in thoughts of loneliness and paid of old age led him to all of its movements and

Dirk Bogarde as Gustav von Ashenbach in Death in Venice.

mannerisms. He became the person Thomas Mann described. Physical representation led to the emotional result.

Why Did You Decide to Be an Actor?

Stop for a moment now to ask why you have taken unto yourself the actor's life. Is it solely for fame and fortune, since those two goals come to too few? Or is it another aspect of acting: the pure enjoyment of acting? What is there about acting that creates enjoyment? It is the opportunity to escape from everyday life, erasing one identity and shaping another.

You submerge yourself not only for the audience's pleasure and approbation, but for yourself. That which you cannot do, or fear to do, is possible when speaking and acting through another person. Therefore you can be fearless or cringing, vulgar or haughty, mean or gentle, all in public, without it reflecting upon yourself personally. If it is something you would within your own core wish to be, you are free to accomplish when plunging into a new character — even an abhorrent one. Is it not also the desire to create and to feel the stirring of another entity within you and the need to bring it to full fruition? Whatever the reason, the total picture of the new individual cannot be brought to life without the costume and make-up to serve as your color to complete the animated portrait. The costume helps to cast that spell of enchantment over the actor, for an actor cannot create magic if he does not feel magical himself.

Every participant in the theatre exists for you alone. Playwright, director, scenic designer, costume designer, wig maker, make-up person, lighting technicians, wardrobe people, stagehands — the theatre itself — all are devoted to conceiving elements which exist for you, and you must take all of these ingredients of other people's artistry and combine them with your own. The audience is waiting.

155

Chapter 16
IMPROVISING A
REHEARSAL COSTUME

How did well-known entertainers develop their performances that were so integrated with costumes and props? Only
through imaginative improvisation.

Costume improvisation is an inherent reflex, and the first
costumes man improvised consisted of leaves and grass. The
Hawaiian hula skirt remains a classic example of early improvised
costuming. Animal skins and other products of nature became
rudimentary costumes, and the American Indian availed himself
of animal horns and multicolored feathers.

Remember as a child when you "play-acted" and eventually
it set you to dreaming and longing to become an actor? Do you
recall how you put together a costume from what you found around
the house and, thus inspired by that improvised costume, you
acted out your assumed role? You know how well that worked
and stirred your imagination.

Because the costume is an essential ingredient to your private preparation prior to attendance at rehearsals and the actual
costume is rarely available while you are developing your role,
costume improvisation comes to your rescue.

As an actor, you don't have to be told how acting improvisation improves your skill, how exciting it is to find your character
taking firmer shape as ideas begin to flow, and the improvisation
continues to take on greater dimensions of the newly discovered
personality.

Improvisation Helps You Experience Actuality

Costume improvisation can do the same while you are im-
pressing upon yourself the lines and character development. It is
not only for acquiring the ease you will feel in the actual costume,
but it allows you to experience the actuality of the individual you
are to represent.

Just as you use your imagination when you improvise lines, it will stretch even further when you build your own "at home" costume. If you need a cape or a skirt, with your wonderful inventiveness you will find that a tablecloth will be a perfect substitute. A towel draped about your head will serve as a hat or a turban. A bed sheet can become a skirt with a train, or it can suffice as a toga. As mentioned before, shoes are important in characterization, and high heels to army boots are all easily accessible as part of your costume improvisation. You know what improvisation is; just use your creative talent in one more direction.

In the course of rehearsal, these ad-libbed bits of costume can be of enormous help to you. Since they have already contributed toward contouring your role at home, your whipped-up clothing will carry you along still further in rehearsal. The costumes of all the actors have an influence upon each other, and even improvised ones can reinforce the interaction between all of you. They prepare each actor toward that day when you see one another in your entire ensembles and lessen the feeling of strangeness. Then the authentic costume will serve as the completed picture which you have already sketched.

Even if the final costume does not exactly approach what you thought it might be, you are nevertheless fully prepared to make those adjustments, since the basics have already been acquired by you. From your improvised costume you have learned to walk in high heels or be graceful in a long skirt; you have acquired the ability to be dashing in a cape or to handle a cane with the proper panache.

Lynn Fontanne and Ellen Terry

Lynn Fontanne received her first acting lessons from Ellen Terry, one of which concerned the value of an improvised costume.

In order to teach her to walk with style in a long skirt, Ellen Terry pinned a bed sheet around her and allowed it to trail behind. With this improvised skirt entirely covering her legs, the unaccustomed feeling gave Lynn Fontanne the fear of falling over it. After being reassured that she would not, she walked with self-confidence, aware of the fact that the sheet now automatically flowed gracefully away from her legs as she moved. Catching on to the trick of walking with poise in a sheet-turned-skirt, she acquired the knack of gesture and posturing in long gowns with beauty and graciousness.

Improvisation doesn't end with rehearsal or with the actual costume. The same actor might wear the identical garments two consecutive evenings and yet be affected differently. He might find that he tilted his hat more effectively the second night to achieve what he discovered to be typical of the character, perhaps suddenly clarifying to himself what the playwright and director wanted him to achieve.

Chapter 17
THE DRESS REHEARSAL

After the cast has been chosen, the theatre selected, the play read to the assembled cast, director and producer, with the costume and scenic designers present as well, rehearsals begin. There are several weeks of devoted, constant work. When necessary, lines are rewritten by the playwright and the direction is changed. The actors work diligently to perfect new lines and carry out constantly changing stage business under the director's guidance. Most particularly the actors are dedicated to delving deeply into the characters they are attempting to bring into being, to create depth to their portrayals, struggling to understand each nuance of people into whom they wish to breathe life. Then, often at the last minute, a performer will come to the costume designer and ask: "What do I wear?" Just that — giving little or no thought as to the costume's influence upon his acting.

Eventually the actors are sent up to a particular costume establishment for fittings before the play is ready for dress rehearsal. At that juncture the producer and director feel that in this ultimate getting it all together for the total picture, they are all set for dress parade and dress rehearsal.

The Total Effect of Costume, Props and Lighting

The most exciting period before the opening is when the actor hears the words "dress rehearsal." It is the interval for the playwright, director, costume, scenic and lighting designers to observe the appearance of the costumes in front of the scenery, how they should be lighted, and the ways in which the actors move in costume. The wigs, hats, character props and accessories such as jewelry, a cane, a fan, a handkerchief — all this adds to the visual description of a character — must be determined in consideration of how they will all work together. Frequently, at the last minute, the actor is told to go over some bit of business with a particular prop on the final set. This may even occur before a dress rehearsal audience to get the feel of the action in order to handle a prop correctly.

161

The thoughtful producer and director know that the effectiveness of their efforts is also dependent upon the thorough ease of the company in their costumes. Ideally, there should be allowed ample time in dress rehearsal for an actor to feel at home in his costume. To be able to move correctly in it, to understand all its possibilities, is to know that it is just as much part of him as his lines. However, in the interest of economy, little time is available for dress rehearsal, and the last-minute enthusiasm of the actor for his costume, coupled with his discovery of its opportunities and challenges, is not enough.

Things Change When the Entire Cast is in Costume

The dress rehearsal is an invigorating event, when the actor sees himself and his fellow actors in complete costume for the first time. It is at this point when all the difficulties of characterization, that "hump" the actor must climb over to fully understand his part, are met with a new understanding. The newly acquired costumes become the last pieces in the jigsaw puzzle, and suddenly the fully revealed character appears. New ideas begin tumbling into the actor's head for his interpretation when he feels the hat on his head, the boots on his feet, the jabot at his throat, the handkerchief in his hand. But the show is about to open, and the sense of much to accomplish in so little time begins to overwhelm him. Furthermore, he suddenly is aware that the actors around him have also become new and different people, and his relationship with them, now that they are in costume, takes on a different aspect.

There is never enough rehearsal time in costume for the actor to realize its influence on his performance. Preview performances are no substitute. The actor has not perfected his role until he has worked a sufficient length of time in the clothing of the character and understands its contribution to his performance. Therefore, it is up to the actor to take the responsibility upon himself to work properly in his costume, to be aware of it in relation to his role. It will affect his posture, his movement, timing, and his concept of the character. With limited dress rehearsal time, in order to do justice to himself and the role, he must do his own homework.

Walter Houston

When Walter Houston was rehearsing his role of the peg-legged Peter Stuyvesant in *Knickerbocker Holiday* by Maxwell Anderson and Kurt Weill, he immediately recognized the special challenge he faced, and asked that he be allowed to work with the peg leg in private. When dress rehearsal day arrived, his costume included a silver peg leg, a long cape and a sword. To everyone's astonishment, he proficiently climbed up and down stairs, thumped across stage, twirled around, pivoting on that silver leg. His right leg was strapped to his thigh, and he expertly concealed it by continually swirling his long cape, which was extended in the back by his sword.

He obviously did his homework and completely perfected his movements in costume long before dress rehearsal and opening night. No last-minute worries for him. Can you imagine the problems he would have faced had he waited until dress rehearsal to be presented with and confronted by his costume? And how could he have truly come to grips with Peter Stuyvesant at all without prior familiarity with his costume?

The costume *persuades* the actor and the audience of the believability of the character. As an actor, when do *you* begin to utilize and understand the costume in relation to your own acting?

Chapter 18
STEPS TO THE STAGE
A Check List

With costume as your partner, together you take twenty-two steps to the stage:

Step One

Be enthusiastic. Enthusiasm is the foundation of all creative art.

Step Two

Exercise your imagination to its fullest capacity.

Step Three

If you are familiar with the part for which you are auditioning, attend the audition in clothing suitable to the role. If you are not auditioning for any specific part, wear clothing or an accessory that will single you out from others; perhaps a scarf or sweater in a striking color or pattern. You will then be both memorable and easily identifiable. When you are called back, wear the identical clothes you wore at the first audition. If you wear other garments, you may not be recognized nor your performance easily recollected. (Refer to Chapter 14: The Audition.)

Step Four

While you are studying your script, form a mental picture of all the roles as well as your own. Fully identify your character, building a biographical background to include:

(1) Placement in time.
(2) Ethnic background.
(3) Social position.
(4) Economic standing.
(5) Home environment.
(6) Location of play's action and character's capacity in those surroundings.

After you have determined the identifying background, begin your detective work to find a visual model for your character. Clothing is the clue. Begin your search for:

(1) Historical events and political aspects of the age.

(2) Prevalent fashions.

(3) Posture of the period.

(4) Style of clothing the character wears in relation to the era and his position in life.

(5) The type of fabric and choice of color you envision is suitable to the role. (Refer to Chapter 5: Fabric, Color and Lighting.)

(6) Posture of individual in respect to his clothing and status.

(7) Style of clothing, type of fabric and choice of color you envision is suitable to other characters' clothing.

(8) Furnishings of the time and place.

(9) Prevalent literature, music and dance.

Sources for research:

(a) Museums

(b) Libraries

(c) Movies

(d) Television

(e) Observation

(Refer to Chapter 2: Research.)

Step Five

Improvise a costume at home, utilizing the information you have gathered in research. Wear the improvised costume as you continue to study the script and learn your lines. (Refer to Chapter 16: Improvising a Rehearsal Costume.)

Step Six

Consult the costume designer. If you are in a contemporary play, inquire whether the costume will be designed or purchased, and what the designer is proposing as to style, fabric and color. If available, request to see a costume sketch so that you may improvise simulated garments.

If you are in a period play, in addition to noting the costume sketch and acquiring information concerning fabric and color, ask if you may have a mockup, or some part of the costume that you know will require adeptness in performance.

In both instances, ascertain the type of shoes you will be wearing and request that you be provided with them in advance. If that cannot be accomplished, make every effort to find a pair as similar as possible. Follow the identical steps for every change of outfit. Each costume has its own mood and portrayal. (Refer to Chapter 15: Rehearsal and Preparation.)

Step Seven

Inquire whether any of the clothing will be restrictive so that you may determine if you will be too uncomfortable or your movements hampered. Discuss the weight of the costume. Become aware of any difficulties that could possibly occur in the interaction of your costume with that of your fellow performers. Try to gather as much information as possible so that there will be a minimum of unforeseen problems or surprises. If nothing can be altered, at least you will be prepared to overcome them. (Refer to Chapter 6: Suitability and Comfort.)

Step Eight

With the information supplied to you by the designer, make practical adjustments to your improvised rehearsal costume. If fabric and color cannot be duplicated, obtain a swatch of material to impart to you an element of the emotional reaction it bestows. (Refer to Chapter 5: Fabric, Color and Lighting; Chapter 16: Improvising a Rehearsal Costume.)

Step Nine

To capture the appropriate walk and posture of the person you are portraying, wear character shoes. Rehearse with your costume accessories. They are part of the action and define the character. In addition, adopt for daily wear an accessory or part of the costume to accustom yourself to your new identity. (Refer to Chapter 3: Accessories; Chapter 7: Posture.)

Step Ten

Continue working with your script in conjunction with an improvised rehearsal outfit. Avoid rehearsing in everyday comfortable clothes. There is meaning in your costume as well as your lines. Attire, action and lines must be coordinated. (Refer to Chapter 15: Rehearsal and Preparation.)

Step Eleven

In creating illusion, be prepared to work with special effects. If you are to be completely disguised in a cumbersome costume, contrive your own equally awkward one, working with it to conceive an imaginative performance. All costumes of fantasy demand experimentation in movement and gesture. (Refer to Chapter 12: Fashioning Fantasy.)

Step Twelve

Props are integrated with the action of a performance and require advance preparation. Obtain substitutes for props you will use on stage and work with them to assure ease and familiarity. (Refer to Chapter 4: Props.)

Step Thirteen

Although you have achieved an intimacy with your role and the character's clothing, your visualization of the character is not completed until you have decided upon hair style and facial appearance. What is your mental image of the features of the individual you are portraying? Until it is later determined by a make-up designer, to assist your development of the role, rely upon yourself to improvise your own make-up, even if it is limited to the style in which you rearrange your hair. Should it be left to your own decision, now is the time to construct your disguise. (Refer to Chapter 8: Masks, Make-up and Disguises.)

Step Fourteen

Stand before a mirror in your improvised costume and make-up; your normal posture does not conform with your new appearance. Your next objective is to learn to move, sit and stand in accordance with the dictates of your clothing. (Refer to Chapter 7: Posture.)

Step Fifteen

If your role is comic, costume is integral to your performance. Incorporate your attire with gesture to produce a comedic effect. (Refer to Chapter 9: Comedians and Costume Identities; Chapter 10: Modes in Mime.)

Step Sixteen

If you are performing as a clown and the costume is left to your determination, or you are establishing your own comedy act, you are in complete control of the creation and coordination of the costume. (Refer to Chapter 9: Comedians and Costume Identities; Chapter 10: Modes in Mime; Chapter 11: The Puppet Master; Chapter 3: Accessories; Chapter 5: Fabrics, Color and Lighting; Chapter 8: Masks, Make-up and Disguises.)

Step Seventeen

You are both actor and costumer if you perform as a ventriloquist or puppeteer. Combine all the principles of acting with costume with origination of characters. (Refer to Chapter 2: Research; Chapter 3: Accessories; Chapter 4: Props; Chapter 5: Fabric, Color and Lighting; Chapter 7: Posture; Chapter 8: Masks, Make-up and Disguises; Chapter 10: Modes in Mime; Chapter 11: The Puppet Master; Chapter 12: Fashioning Fantasy.)

Step Eighteen

Both performers of fantasy and dancer's roles are interpreted by mime united with costume. Opera combines the art of singing and acting; exposition of character encompasses voice, acting, mime, fantasy and costume. (Refer to Chapter 10: Modes in Mime; Chapter 12: Fashioning Fantasy; Chapter 2: Research; Chapter 3: Accessories; Chapter 4: Props; Chapter 5: Fabric, Color and Lighting; Chapter 6: Suitability and Comfort; Chapter 7: Posture.)

Step Nineteen

Study yourself in costume before a mirror. Your reflection will familiarize you with the character you are becoming and be your guide in the creation of effective performance. It will enable you to see and react to your acquired personality as others will during the course of your performance. (Refer to Chapter 15: Rehearsal and Preparation.)

Step Twenty

You arrive early for a dress rehearsal to give yourself time to feel comfortable in your costume. You fully understand the emotions of the role, know your lines, and are acclimated to the action. Without your costume, accessories and make-up your char-

169

acter is not yet alive. In wardrobe you will see your costumes. They are attractive to behold, but are only inanimate clothes on hangers. They are waiting to become vitalized. You are anticipating one another, for it is only together will you both come into a unique existence. You are fully prepared to consummate your partnership with your costume. (Refer to Chapter 1: The Inspiration.)

Step Twenty-One

Working with all the components of characterization — research, costume, accessories, props, make-up, disguise, and your mirror — you will have the confidence of a thorough understanding of your role and be fully prepared to effectively convey your interpretation. You will approach dress rehearsal confident in the fact that you and your costume have built together a believable and effective role. (Refer to Chapter 17: The Dress Rehearsal.)

Step Twenty-Two

Opening night has arrived. You are well prepared and ready to go on. Suddenly all stage directions, all acting techniques, all lines are forgotten; you freeze.

Your costume and the mirror will come to your aid. Contemplate your reflection. You are familiar with the individual in the mirrored image, and it is not you. Your personal individuality is irradicated. When you step on stage, keep in mind the likeness in the mirror, with the knowledge that the image you beheld is what you and the audience believe to be true. The costume is your hiding place, and together you have created another personality. You are in it together for a long run. (Refer to Chapter 19: The Finishing Touch.)

Chapter 19
THE FINISHING TOUCH

Even before written history the actor was a figure of importance to the community. As the first storyteller he related familiar events and experiences, his oral tales also bringing wonder and adventure into the surrounding circle of rapt listeners. To effectively inject reality into the stories, the narrator relied solely upon his talent to speak in varying tones and his ability to imitate the appearance and sounds of other creatures. His skill to do so rendered him separate and apart from others. Simple legends grew into chronicles and prose with motion, inviting additional participants with imitative ability to relate them with action as well as words. Constantly developing through the millenniums, those first enactments have evolved into the complex theatre, film and television world of today.

The Actor Is the Focal Point of All Theatre

From unadorned anecdotes of one person to our current multilayered productions, the focal point of it all was, and always will be, the actor. He bears a tremendous responsibility since he serves many functions. The actor, through the character he defines, establishes fantasy worlds into which men, women and children wish to temporarily escape. Theatre, in whatever its form, works through the actor to do more than just entertain. It introduces people to those whom they otherwise would never discover, and to times and events long gone. It presents problems of the past, present and future, asks questions and seeks solutions. Theatre finds a common denominator between men, living or dead. It instills passions and plays upon human emotions. The theatre enables the spectator to withdraw from himself, or to recognize an identification with others; to laugh at someone else's foibles as well as his own; to cry over another's misfortunes and open his own heart and mind.

The instrument necessary to express this great range of the human condition is the actor. Without him the world would be less informed and less inspired. Without the actor there would be less laughter and more indifference to the facets of the life and history of mankind.

The actor has an overwhelmingly important role in life to satisfy all these needs in others. He is the man with the message, whatever it may be, and the dedicated actor devotes himself to delivering that message with the utmost reality in order to make it potent and acceptable. It is an onerous but satisfying task, since it is placed only upon those with a special talent.

The Actor Needs the Help of Others

But the talent must be developed and reinforced in numerous ways in order to bring forth the re-creation of other eras and people, and to introduce circumstances and conditions otherwise unknown. Behind the actor are those who work solely for him to help in that development and reinforcement, and who give him a voice in addition to his own. All the many elements of theatre unite and merge into the complete actor.

Costume Is a Key Component in All Theatre

That part of theatre which is the costume is a buttress to all the performing arts. The circus would have no fun or color without costume. Vaudeville would lose its entertaining glitter; comedy and burlesque would be limited in their scope if the costume were not a component. Lacking costumes, grand opera would cease to be grand. Even the barker at a fair could not create the excitement of enticement to the mystery hidden behind the curtain if there was no identifying costume to invite gazes. Every form of performance is theatre, and there is no theatre without the actor and his costume performing together.

Garson Kanin adapted a French play entitled *Dreyfus In Rehearsal*, which concerned a group of Jews in a small Polish village who were rehearsing a play about Captain Dreyfus. It was a play-within-a-play in which no one was a professional actor, and in rehearsal their acting inabilities were apparent. One of the members of the cast was a tailor, and he assured his fellow amateur actors that their deficiencies and errors would evaporate when they put on their costumes.

In the tailor's view, the costume would make the actor. Of course that is not true. An actor not measuring up to his part

172

might mistakenly rely entirely upon appearance to put over the performance. This is not the attitude of the dedicated, talented actor. He knows that the costume influences his performance and is an adjunct to his acting, not a replacement.

You and Your Costume Act Together

The actor must be *passionate* about every facet of his work. He has need of passion for the costume he wears as well as passion for the text of the play. Enthusiastically embrace the costume as a tool which is intimately involved with your acting. You and your costume act together: you are a team, and there is not much you can do without each other. Remove the costume and you break up the act. Your costume is your friend, your aid, a part of you. The costume is the polish, the finishing touch. You are inextricably bound together. The costume is the performing partner.

Co-author Jac Lewis discusses costume designs with students at the Bureau of Cultural Education Services, Wantagh, Long Island, New York.

Sources

Adachi, Barbara C. *Backstage at Bunraku*. New York: John Weatherhill Inc., 1985.

Anderson, Kenneth G. *Faces, Forms, Films*. South Brunswick and New York: A. S. Barnes and Co., Inc, 1971.

Barrow, Kenneth. *Mr. Chips*. London: Methuen, 1985.

Barton, Lucy. *Appreciating Costume*. Boston: W. H. Baker, 1969.

Beaumont, Cyril W. *The Ballet Called Swan Lake*. New York: Dance Horizons, 1982.

Bentham, Frederick. *The Art of Stage Lighting*. Third Edition, London: Pitman House, 1980.

Bogarde, Dirk. *Snakes and Ladders*. New York: Holt, Rinehart and Winston, 1979, c1978.

Brown, Jared. *The Fabulous Lunts*. New York: Atheneum, 1986.

Buckle, Richard. *Nijinsky*. New York: Simon & Schuster, (c1971).

Butler, Ivan. *Silent Magic*. London: Columbus Books, Limited, 1987.

Callow, Simon. *Being an Actor*. London: Methuen, 1984.

Castle, Charles. *Oliver Messel: A Biography*. New York: Thames and Hudson, 1986.

Cole, Toby and Chinoy, Helen Krich. *Actors on Acting*. Newly Rev. Ed., New York: Crown Publishers, 1970.

Collier, Richard. *Make-Believe: The Magic of International Theatre*. New York: Dodd, Mead & Company, 1986.

Courtney, Marguerite. *Laurette*. New York: Limelight Editions, 1984, c1968.

Craig, David. *On Performing: A Handbook for Actors, Dancers, Singers on the Musical Stage*. New York: McGraw-Hill Book Company, c1987.

Dandridge, Dorothy and Conrad, Earl. *Everything and Nothing; the Dorothy Dandridge Tragedy*. New York: Abelard-Schuman, (1970).

Durant, Will and Ariel. *Rousseau and Revolution*. New York: Simon and Schuster, 1967.

Durant, Will and Ariel. *The Age of Reason Begins*. New York: Simon and Schuster, 1961.

Edwards, Gwynne. *The Discreet Art of Luis Buñuel: a Reading of His Films.* London: Marion Boyars Publishers Inc., 1982.

Evans, Maurice. *All This and Evans Too.* Columbia, S. C.: University of South Carolina Press, c1987.

Gielgud, Sir John. *Early Stages.* New York: Taplinger Publishing Co., New York: Revised Edition, 1974.

Gielgud, Sir John. *An Actor and His Time.* London: Sidgwick & Jackson, 1979.

Goldsmith, Arnold L. *The Golem Remembered 1908-1980: Variations of a Jewish Legend.* Detroit: Wayne State University Press, 1981.

Gordon, Ruth. *My Side.* New York: Harper & Row, 1976.

Hagen, Uta. *Respect for Acting.* New York: Macmillan Publishing Co., 1973

Hale, Alice. *Big River.* Theatre Crafts, Volume 19, Aug./Sept. 1985.

Hayes, Elizabeth R. *A Guide to Dance Production: On With the Show.* Reston, Va.: National Dance Association of the American Alliance for Health, Physical Education and Dance, c1981.

Hoelterhoff, Manuela. *Zefferelli's Glittery "Turandot."* Wall Street Journal, March 27, 1987.

Hogarth, Ann and Bussell, Jan. *Fanfare for Puppets! A Personal and Idiosyncratic View of the Puppet Theatre.* Newton Abbot, Devon; North Pomfret, Vt.: David & Charles, c1985.

Honan, William H. *Transformation Lies at the Very Heart of Inspired Acting.* New York Times, May 11, 1986.

Kalter, Joanmarie. *Actors on Acting: Performing in Theatre and Film Today.* New York: Sterling Publishing Co., c1979.

Logan, Joshua. *Josh. My Up and Down, In and Out Life.* New York: Delacorte Press, c1976; London: W. H. Allen, 1977.

Madden, David. *Harlequin's Stick — Charlie's Cane: A Comparative Study of Commedia dell'arte and Silent Slapstick Comedy.* Bowling Green, Ohio: Bowling Green University Popular Press, c1975.

McCabe, John. *Charlie Chaplin.* Garden City, New York: Doubleday, 1978.

Mazo, Joseph H. *Prime Movers: The Makers of Modern Dance in America.* New York: William Morrow and Company, Inc. c1977.

Murray, Edward. *Fellini the Artist.* New York: Frederick Unger Publishing Co., c1976, c1985.

Newman, Barbara and Spath, Leslie E. *Swan Lake, Sadler's Wells Royal Ballet.* London: Dance Books Ltd., 1983.

Olivier, Laurence. *On Acting.* New York: Simon and Schuster, c1986.

Peters, Margot. *Mrs. Pat: The Life of Mrs. Patrick Campbell.* New York: Knopf: Distributed by Random House, 1984.

Philpott, Alexis Roberts. *Dictionary of Puppetry.* London: MacDonald and Company Ltd., 1969.

Reid, Francis. *The Stage Lighting Handbook.* Second Edition, London: Adam and Charles Black, 1982.

Redgrave, Michael. *In My Mind's Eye.* London: Weidenfeld & Nicolson, 1982

Rolfe, Bari. *Mimes on Miming: Writings on the Art of Mime.* Los Angeles: Panjandrum/Aris Books, (1979).

Sandrow, Nahma. *Surrealism: Theatre, Arts, Ideas.* New York: Harper & Row, (1972).

Skinner, Cornelia Otis. *Family Circle.* Boston: Houghton Mifflin Company, 1948.

Smith, C. Ray, Edited by. *The Theatre Crafts Book of Make-up, Masks, and Wigs.* Emmaus, Pa.: Rodale Press, Inc., (1974).

Strindberg, August. Edwin Bjorkman Translation *Plays by August Strindberg.* Foreword to *Miss Julia.* Revised Edition. New York: Charles Scribner's Sons, 1920.

Vickers, Hugo. *Cecil Beaton: An Authorized Biography.* London: Weidenfeld and Nicolson, c1985.

Vox, Valentine. *I Can See Your Lips Moving. The History and Art of Ventriloquism.* Tadworth, Surrey: Kaye & Ward, 1981.

Walker, Kathrine Sorley. *Eyes on Mime: Language Without Speech.* New York: John Day Company, (1969).

Webster, Margaret. *The Same Only Different: Five Generations of a Great Theatre Family.* New York: Knopf, 1969.

Webster, Margaret. *Don't Put Your Daughter on the Stage.* New York: Alfred A. Knopf, 1972.

Wilk, Max. *The Golden Age of Television: Notes From the Survivors.* New York: Delacorte Press, c1976.

Wilson, Edwin. *Theatre: Of Relations Erotic and Diplomatic.* Wall Street Journal, March 22, 1988.

Zinder, David G. *The Surrealist Connection: An Approach to a Surrealist Aesthetic of Theatre.* Ann Arbor, Mich.: UMI Research Press, c1980.

Zolotow, Maurice. *Stagestruck.* New York: Harcourt, Brace & World Inc., 1964, 1965.

Index

ABOUT THE AUTHORS

MIRIAM STRIEZHEFF LEWIS

Though the field of law has been Miriam Striezheff Lewis' principal livelihood, she has also maintained a sideline career as a writer in several specialty areas, aided by her study of literature and writing at Northwestern University.

Devoted as well to opera and theatre, she has studied both in Europe and the United States. As a result of a lifetime of theatre appreciation, she developed a keen interest in the transformation of a playscript into stage reality. With this study she has discovered the importance of costume as the actor's performing partner.

This knowledge and her writing skills were a dovetail fit with her husband's profession as a costume designer. When they retired to Chapel Hill, North Carolina, they decided to combine their talents to produce a book defining this special aspect of theatre performance.

Currently, Mrs. Lewis is working on a novel about a woman whose life is altered by a theatrical performance.

JAC LEWIS

Coming from a family with theatrical ties, young Jac was fascinated by his famous comedian uncles Danny and George P. Murphy who performed in the days of vaudeville. Influenced also by his grandfather, a fashion designer, Jac Lewis was inevitably drawn into the fields of theatrical costume and fashion design in his adult working life.

After graduating from the Philadelphia College of Art, Mr. Lewis began his career with two theatrical fabric companies. During this time, two books of his costume designs were published for dance schools throughout the United States. He later joined the Eaves Costume Company in New York as a staff designer.

Mr. Lewis designed special costumes for the Schubert organization's performances of plays and operettas. Many actors wore his creations, including Danny Kaye, Doris Day, Perry Como, Kaye Starr, Donald Cook, and other famous names.

For a number of years Mr. Lewis maintained his own fashion salon in New York City. He was also Costume Advisor to the High School of Performing Arts in Manhattan which was featured in the movie and TV series *Fame*. It was at this school that the author first lectured on the relation of costume to performance, thus formulating the idea for *COSTUME: THE PERFORMING PARTNER*.